SAGE was founded in 1965 by Sara Miller McCune to support the dissemination of usable knowledge by publishing innovative and high-quality research and teaching content. Today, we publish over 900 journals, including those of more than 400 learned societies, more than 800 new books per year, and a growing range of library products including archives, data, case studies, reports, and video. SAGE remains majority-owned by our founder, and after Sara's lifetime will become owned by a charitable trust that secures our continued independence.

Los Angeles | London | New Delhi | Singapore | Washington DC | Melbourne

Advance Praise

'An interesting, engaging and empowering read that guides one through the fast-evolving retail landscape. *Retail Beyond Detail* journeys through one of the oldest industries, as it delves deeper into what defines it, makes it and even breaks it. The book—through its quick tips and relatable examples—makes it a perfect "go-to" for those passionate about stepping into the retail industry and understanding it better. The wide gamut of topics conveyed through a mix of story-telling, examples and explanation make this a great resource for anyone who really wants to be a meaningful player within this industry.'

Rakesh Biyani, *Joint Managing Director, Future Retail Ltd*

'Indian retail is always talked about as the next big opportunity. In reality, it continues to be an intriguing and challenging Ali Baba's cave due to its diversity of customers and products. Gibson's book is a primer on the DNA of Indian retail, which explains the opportunities and challenges along with success stories of operational excellence. A must-read for all retailers and students to unravel the secret sauce of success, while achieving customer centricity, co-existence and profitability.'

Govind Shrikhande, *Customer Care Associate and Former Managing Director, Shoppers' Stop Ltd*

'In the context of India, whenever there is reference to retailing, it is common to equate it to modern trade. However, having practised it for several decades, I can say that the core of Indian retailing still remains largely undiscovered. How can small enterprises survive for so many years? My dear friend Gibson has touched the nerve that will be torchlight to seekers of the truth of Indian retailing. Interesting!'

K. Radhakrishnan, *Co-founder, Tata Starquik.com*

'This book is a power-packed capsule on retail. It captures the science of modern retailing as practised by big successful retailers in India and across the world and blends them with the unique practices of the small mom and pop retailers that have made them successful. It weaves both these strands into a comprehensive guide to retailing that is full of examples, heart-warming stories and practical ways to implement. Gibson has demystified modern retail for the family retailers and for the large retailers, he has brought out the practices of the family retailers which build unparalleled stickiness and resilience. In doing so, it also makes for a fascinating and lovely read for a consumer and a practitioner.'

Neelesh Hundekari, *Partner (Asia Pacific)–Consumer and Retail Practice, A.T. Kearney Ltd, UK (India branch office)*

'The right book at the right time—when Indian retail is at its crossroads.'

Hemu Ramaiah, *Former CEO and Founder, Landmark Book Stores; Managing Director, Shop4solutions Pvt. Ltd*

'If an attitude of positivity and genuine friendliness is shown by every shopkeeper, they can get closer to their customers and win them forever. Gibson's book gives useful pointers to run the retail business in India profitably—whether big or small, or traditional or modern! It's an interesting and resourceful read, page after page, with case examples and illustrations. I'm sure every reader would be delighted to go through each winning experience in the world of retailing presented in the book!'

Rajeev Gopalakrishnan, *President–South Asia, Bata Emerging Markets*

'The awareness levels of most leading brands are very high. So, mass media channels no more play a significant role in brand purchase decisions. The focus now shifts to the retail outlet—the point-of-purchase. The more you understand the retail environment, the better you will succeed in building strong brands. Gibson's book beacons it all!'

Biju Dominic, *CEO and Co-founder, FinalMile Consulting (Behaviour Architects)*

'Dr Gibson is an extremely experienced retail professional, who is also endowed with the gift of extraordinary writing and teaching skills, which enable him to share his knowledge with others. The 10 success factors will help small retail businesses survive and thrive the disruption that will unfold during the next decade.'

Krish Iyer, *President and CEO, Walmart India*

'This book is a great read filled with valuable detailed information hand-picked from Indian retail for Indian retail. The curated selection of real-life learning from the best of great traditional and modern retailers adds authenticity to the different concepts explained by Gibson in the journey of the book. Interesting anecdotes from his life experiences add delightful "beyond detail" nostalgia to the descriptions and add a very important ingredient in retail—the emotional touch. The book gives very useful and hands-on tips derived from intuitive traditional shopkeeping interpreted in the context of today's competitive, connected world of retail in India. A superb read and a valuable ready reckoner for efficient and effective retailing!'

Surender Gnanaolivu, *Senior Consultant–Retail Experience*

'Gibson's book is a capsule of curated retailing knowledge. It will be immensely useful for retailers and associates in retail. The book covers complex topics in a very simple manner and hence would be useful for the uninitiated too.'

Kumar Rajagopalan, *CEO, Retailers Association of India*

Retail
BEYOND
Detail

Retail BEYOND Detail

The Great Indian Retailing Business

Gibson G. Vedamani

 |

Los Angeles | London | New Delhi
Singapore | Washington DC | Melbourne

Copyright © Gibson G. Vedamani, 2018

All rights reserved. No part of this book may be reproduced or utilised in any form or by any means, electronic or mechanical, including photocopying, recording or by any information storage or retrieval system, without permission in writing from the publisher.

First published in 2018 by

SAGE Publications India Pvt Ltd
B1/I-1 Mohan Cooperative Industrial Area
Mathura Road, New Delhi 110 044, India
www.sagepub.in

SAGE Publications Inc
2455 Teller Road
Thousand Oaks, California 91320, USA

SAGE Publications Ltd
1 Oliver's Yard, 55 City Road
London EC1Y 1SP, United Kingdom

SAGE Publications Asia-Pacific Pte Ltd
3 Church Street
#10-04 Samsung Hub
Singapore 049483

Published by Vivek Mehra for SAGE Publications India Pvt Ltd, typeset in 11/14.25 pts Adobe Caslon Pro by Fidus Design Pvt. Ltd., Chandigarh and printed at Saurabh Printers Pvt Ltd, Greater Noida.

Library of Congress Cataloging-in-Publication Data
Name: Vedamani, Gibson G., author.
Title: Retail beyond detail: the great Indian retailing business / Gibson G. Vedamani.
Description: New Delhi, India: SAGE Publications India, 2018. | Includes bibliographical references.
Identifiers: LCCN 2018022467 (print) | LCCN 2018024201 (ebook) | ISBN 9789352807611
    (Web PDF) | ISBN 9789352807604 (E pub 2.0) | ISBN 9789352807598 (pbk.: alk. paper)
Subjects: LCSH: Retail trade—India.
Classification: LCC HF5429.6.I5 (ebook) | LCC HF5429.6.I5 V46 2018 (print) |
    DDC 381/.10954—dc23
LC record available at https://lccn.loc.gov/2018022467

ISBN: 978-93-528-0759-8 (PB)

SAGE Team: Manisha Mathews, Sandhya Gola, Ashmita Ahuja and Rajinder Kaur

To the millions of traditional retailers of India, who toil on the shop floors, day in and day out, to satisfy customers!

A traditional retailer in India is more often a friend to every family in the catchment than a mere shopkeeper.

He is an integral part of the family to many of his customers!

He sells, gives credit and even runs small errands for his customers!

He is so trustworthy that he is sometimes the custodian of the house keys of the family, when the number of nuclear family members outnumbers the number of keys to the door!

His store often readily doubles up as safe haven for the neighbourhood children when they come back from school before their parents return home!

He is not a passing cloud, but a lasting phenomenon in INDIA!

Thank you for choosing a SAGE product!
If you have any comment, observation or feedback,
I would like to personally hear from you.

Please write to me at **contactceo@sagepub.in**

Vivek Mehra, Managing Director and CEO, SAGE India.

Bulk Sales

SAGE India offers special discounts
for purchase of books in bulk.
We also make available special imprints
and excerpts from our books on demand.

For orders and enquiries, write to us at

Marketing Department
SAGE Publications India Pvt Ltd
B1/I-1, Mohan Cooperative Industrial Area
Mathura Road, Post Bag 7
New Delhi 110044, India

E-mail us at **marketing@sagepub.in**

Get to know more about SAGE

Be invited to SAGE events, get on our mailing list.
Write today to **marketing@sagepub.in**

This book is also available as an e-book.

Contents

FOREWORD *BY HARISH BIJOOR*		xi
PREFACE		xiii
ACKNOWLEDGEMENTS		xvii

SECTION I:	**GLIMPSES OF THE INTRINSIC INDIAN RETAILING**	**1**
Chapter 1:	India's Unique Retail Evolution	3
Chapter 2:	The Significance of Micro, Small and Medium Enterprise (MSME) Retailing in India	12
Chapter 3:	The Diversity of Indian Consumers and Consumption	19
Chapter 4:	Factors Fuelling Retail Growth in India	28
Chapter 5:	The Hurdles That Retailers Face in India	34
Chapter 6:	FDI in Retailing: Is It Threatening?	41
Chapter 7:	Foreign or Indian, Big Retailers Pose the Same Threat	51
Chapter 8:	The Changing Face of Retail Communication	60
Chapter 9:	Disruptions and Innovations in Indian Retailing	69
Chapter 10:	India's Rapid Adoption of Online Retailing	77

SECTION II:	TEN SUCCESS SECRETS TO WIN	87
Secret 1:	Be Determined to Win	89
	Blending Intelligence with Determination: Khadim's, Kolkata	96
Secret 2:	Choose the Right Location	100
	Starting Small: Hatti Food and Beverages Pvt. Ltd (Hatti Kaapi), Bengaluru	108
Secret 3:	Know Your Customers	118
	Understanding Customers Thoroughly: MSH Sarees Pvt. Ltd (Jashn Brand of Retail Stores), Mumbai	124
Secret 4:	Organize Store Space Efficiently	131
	Scaling Up from a Sidewalk Hawking Space: A. P. Mani & Sons, Mumbai	138
Secret 5:	Stock up the Store for Profit	144
	Right Product Strategies: Patanjali Ayurved Limited, Haridwar	154
Secret 6:	Optimize Store Operations	159
	Ensuring Operational Excellence: Viveks Limited, Chennai	166
Secret 7:	Ensure Financial Discipline	173
	Hard Work and Zero Debt: Sethwala Foods Limited, Mumbai	180
Secret 8:	Adopt Simple Store Systems	185
	Rewrite Rules; Retain Values: Future Group, Mumbai	188
Secret 9:	Promote the Store	192
	Baking Tasty Recipes for Her Consumers: The Sugarr & Spice, Kolkata	201

Secret 10:	Place the Right People in the Store	205
	Choosing the Right People and Practices: Shri Kannan Departmental Store, Coimbatore	211

BIBLIOGRAPHY 217

ABOUT THE AUTHOR 220

Foreword

Retail is a world in itself. Possibly older than the oldest known profession to date.

There is a little bit of retail in everything we see, touch, smell, taste and experience. To that extent, retail is a sensorial part of our everyday life. Everything that is bought or sold reaches out to us through this very intermediary process called retail. Every marketplace, physical or digital, is retail. And every enterprise, whether it be an economic, commercial, religious, political or social, markets itself through this intermediary. Retail is that point where the buyer meets the seller. And there is a seller everywhere, just as there is a buyer everywhere in society.

India then is a nation of shopkeepers. We boast a total of 14.6 million retail outlets that cater to a population that nudges the 1.3 billion mark. The ratio of a retail outlet to a set of human beings in India is a very robust and healthy one. And if there are 14.6 million retail outlets of every size, varying from a size of 1 to a size of 400 employees, this must be a very involved business. A business that contributes to the lives of more than 75 million Indians in a rather direct manner of income generation and use!

Retail, therefore, touches every human being there is. If you are a consumer, you are touched by the tentacles of retail. If you are a marketer, you are a part of this enterprise to make a living. Retail is undeniably India's biggest business enterprise in terms of sheer numbers of people involved in it.

A nation of micro-retail enterprises that thrived in the cubbyhole shops that were not even 'mom and pop stores', but were instead solo enterprises of the enterprising, progressively got populated by mom and pop stores, department stores, organized retail chains and e-retail with a cusp presence in both the physical and digital retail worlds. The beauty of variegated India is the fact that each of these types of retail continue to thrive in India.

Gibson Vedamani does a good job of peeking into a fair bit of each of these types. His vision is not clouded by modern retail of the organized format. Instead, he peeks into the small and beautiful as well. Gibson picks key success factors in this thriving space, and makes cases out of the big and small successes of Indian retail. Gibson contributes enough detailing to satiate the hunger of a student in quest of learning, as equally a retail owner in quest of wanting to improve and change. To that extent, the cases Gibson presents are packed with good learning.

As I ran through the cases, I could literally smell the place and the fervour of the retail point. As someone who has 'been there' and 'done that', Gibson now 'writes that'! Nice! Way to go!

Harish Bijoor
Brand Expert and Founder
Harish Bijoor Consults Inc.

Preface

The famous adage of retailing is 'Retail is Detail'. I have been an advocate of the power of positive thinking. I know by my experience that retail goes beyond detail. Touching the very hearts of customers is one of the major arts of the retail business. Even those little things attended to by retailers from their traditions do work wonders to establish a good relationship with customers. That is typical of the characteristic DNA of Indian retailers. This book showcases a few of the tacit 'tacts' of traditionalism that go beyond the explicit details of the business, which can win over modernism if practised thoughtfully for the benefit of the customers!

Fear is a factor that brings setback to those intending to do the retail business and it may pull them back from doing it, for sure. So, many people toe the safer line of being employed in retail organizations. Fear of failure in business may loom large before some and hamper them from taking even the first step of getting into a business! What is missing with the people engaged with large retailers as employees is the entrepreneurial passion. On the other hand, entrepreneurs who are engaged in the small and medium-sized retail business in India are seen to be quite successful businessmen. They often combine the strengths of entrepreneurship and customer centricity with operational professionalism. Not only do they excel but they also thwart competition from the large players and multinationals to win in the competitive retail business in India.

This book is an attempt to inspire as many as possible and to help them take to the business of retailing in any form. They only must have the eagerness to do a few things right at the right value in the right time and in the right locations, which many may not relate to. The secrets discussed in the book for ensuring successful retailing include the time-tested rights of the business. Small merchants and retailers in India have made it to be successful, fighting against big players. They work with a few tricks up their sleeves. Some small businessmen take advantage of the growth of big retailers and partner with them in progress. They work with clear strategic intents! Some small retailers take shelter under the big ones who bring more customers to the very location that helps every other business in the region to be successful. They have the knack of creating the same feathers to flock together!

Everyone appreciates Uber, who is in the big business of transportation of the public by cab service worldwide without owning a single cab! And that is the power of an idea! An Ola effortlessly replicated the idea in India successfully and gives Uber itself the run for its money in India today! Maybe someone has a small store and I am trying to sensitize such store owners to do well and to motivate/facilitate them to act fearlessly irrespective of the entry of foreign or big retailers. I am emphasizing the fact that retailers can win with the optimization of their latent efficiencies, talents and skills so that they can offer customers quality of merchandise and service at affordable prices. Further, this book illustrates the ways and means of how even our smallest traditional businesses can excel amidst the threats that may be there in the marketplace from large retailers.

The first section focuses on the opportunities that exist in India for the growth of the retailing business while discussing the plight of small- and medium-sized retailers and how they can build a successful retail business. The second section explains in detail the ways to achieve store operating excellence and make profits. There are 10 chosen success secrets discussed in detail, which capture the very essence of victory with relevant illustrations the readers can relate to. From their humble beginnings—from being employees or small merchants themselves—a few people have made it big in their retail business efforts. The second section includes such 10 inspiring case illustrations of entrepreneurs, attaining a humongous growth, making their way 'from surviving in the lowly streets to studding the high streets'! Thank you for choosing to read this book of inspirational retail anecdotes and illustrations.

For those passionate aspirers who can gather the gall to pick up the hard stones of efforts and build their own steps to climb the pinnacle of success, I am sure this book would be a great treat!

Happy reading!

Acknowledgements

I thank my Lord and Saviour Jesus Christ who has been my prayer-answering God Almighty, enabling fulfilment of all my dreams. This book is yet another proof of such fulfilment.

During the course of my writing this book, I interacted with many small retailers who willingly discussed with me their experiences, successes and even their pain areas, and I thank all of them from the bottom of my heart.

I express my profound gratitude to those successful retail entrepreneurs whom I spoke with personally for this book, Mr Nagesh Nadar, Mr T. Thanushgaran, Mr B. A. Kodandarama Setty, Mr Mudar Sethwala, Mr Chander Jashnani and Mr U. S. Mahendar. They shared willingly and enthusiastically the details of their journey towards achieving success, which, I am sure, will serve as good lessons for many upcoming retailers to follow.

The art creative team at Think WhyNot (TYN), Mumbai (www.thinkwhynot.com), made special illustrations for this book. I place on record my appreciation for each member of the team.

Last but not the least, my heartfelt gratitude goes to all the members of my family who inspire me in my pursuits and endeavours.

SECTION I

Glimpses of the Intrinsic Indian Retailing

India's Unique Retail Evolution

CHAPTER 1

[*The Indian retail business landscape is wide enough for every shopkeeper, whether small or big, to serve customers and grow.*]

Retailing in India has come a long way. The evolution of Indian retailing began centuries ago, when farmers exchanged one kind of goods for another, in the barter system. The showcasing of goods aggregated from various farms within an accessible radius in a central shandy market location on a weekly basis became popular, where items from vegetables to cattle were traded. In a revenue district, many shandy markets would meet on days that do not clash in the vicinity so that people could visit these markets conveniently. Each weekly market had its significance and specialization. Some markets were popular for farm produce, some for cattle and some for other varieties of goods. Every market had its own entertainment and local snack specialties and so people often enjoyed the whole day shopping and having fun. On a parallel scale, the wholesale markets developed in towns, and these became the feeder markets for various smaller towns and villages. Grains and grocery were traded in India with the help of agents, and an agent is the middleman who

[Since coexistence is a virtue and customer preferences and tastes in India are a mix of traditional and modern, all forms of retailing have a promising future only if they can add value to consumers.]

negotiates the price with aggregated farmers for his customers who may be from faraway places too. The middleman would take a small percentage of the commission such as a per cent or two, on the transaction. In villages and small towns, shops emerged in high streets, and each location had a busy shopping high street filled with various kinds of small shops such as kirana, spices store, ready-made garment store and variety gift store. The nearby town's wholesale feeder markets catered to these shops, sometimes on credit too. For all the popular fast-moving consumer goods (FMCG) companies, these wholesale markets were significant, and in towns, the FMCG companies appointed distributors to supply to wholesalers and some significant retailers. The distributors serviced other smaller retailers. In India, markets being widely spread, the distribution system played a very effective role. The principle of trade was based on the concept: The more the distribution, the more the sale and, hence, the more the consumption.

A Shandy Market

Clothing material and textile retailing in India saw a new high in the form of brands when the textile revolution took place in the late 1960s and through the 1970s. Textile brands such as Binny, Bombay Dyeing, Gwalior, Morarjee, S. Kumars, Vimal and Raymond gained significance on a highlighted plane on the shelves and signages of various textile shops across India. Branded textile dealership stores emerged on Indian high streets, including those in villages too. At the same time, 'sarees' were branded as well, often associating the name with each variety's origin such as Kancheevaram and Pochampalli and the man-made fibre sarees came to be known by brand names. Some sarees were branded based on the names of hit movies! In the early 1990s, modern retailing evolved.

Many grocery stores selling only grains and masalas grew bigger into kirana stores with added merchandise categories of brand products sold by FMCG companies and with value-added, cleaned and repacked grains and food products. While grocery stores weighed and packed products in used newspapers with jute strings, the emerging kirana stores repacked products in ready measures in sealed poly bags. A big brand proliferation followed in all the categories of merchandise—more significantly in apparel and food categories. Lifestyle products too have seen branding in a big way. After liberalization in 1991, department stores were the first to spring up followed by supermarkets and then by hypermarkets. Simultaneously, by the late 1990s and early 2000s, malls came up fast in cities such as Mumbai, Delhi, NCR region and Bengaluru and a little later in other metros.

Coexistence_ The Indian Retail Virtue

In the Western developed economies, various changes took place in the evolutionary process. As stores evolved, shopping zones were created which made local catchment retailers relocate to the new zones. As store formats became larger in size, the small stores vanished. In every step of retail evolution, the older forms of retailing became extinct. India's retail evolution is extremely unique. In all the aforementioned phases of the evolution process, except the barter system, we have all the early and traditional forms of retailing still intact. We have weekly markets in villages, and we have the old traditional small stores in villages and small towns as well. Even after so many new modern stores have come into existence, smaller stores have been found to redefine and reorient themselves for the better. Since coexistence is a virtue and customer preferences and tastes in India are a mix of traditional and modern, all forms of retailing have a promising future only if they can add value to consumers. The Indian landscape is wide enough for every retailer—whether small or big, or online or brick and mortar—to serve customers with what they need and want, and grow in the process.

My Tryst with Shandy and Flea Markets

As school teachers, both my grandfather and grandmother spent the maximum part of their career in rural areas. It was often fun and mirth for me to go with my grandfather for shopping and a lot of excitement to go with him on hunting. Clipping a BSA double barrel rifle to his bicycle, he used to take me along, as he went about hunting. It was quite a thrill to see him hunt. It was more interesting for me when he took me shopping in the village weekly market. I could get my instant gratification from the sweets and eats he used to buy for me. The market was an open place, and it was fun to see him bargaining and later boasting with my grandmother about how he managed to win good bargains!

I was driving through the highway from Pune to Bengaluru recently, and in a village near Satara, I came across a similar weekly open market that caught my attention. There it was, the same kind of market with open shops under shanties selling various kinds of merchandise. My car automatically slowed down to catch a glimpse of the market (more like Nirad Chaudhuri's car that is driven by sheer will power!). I realized that shandy markets are still commonplace in India. Temporary structures are erected every week in a marketplace to enable the farmers and other small retailers to spread their wares and retail in a street retail format.

A weekly market covers many catchment villages from where customers would come and shop their weekly needs; the shops would range from those of small appliances, garments, masalas and vegetables to selling cattle and fodder too. 'Bargaining' is an integral part of the shandy market where retailers quote their prices for commodities and wares and customers seek the pleasure of hunting for good bargains. In these markets even cows, buffaloes, sheep and goats are sold. Prices are negotiated symbolically using a system of the buyer asking for the price by touching the fingers of the seller under a cloth cover so that the negotiation is kept confidential in the open market. Similarly, fairs and melas in villages are an annual phenomenon, and they are usually organized during religious and temple festivals. Shopping, eating out and entertainment are the key components of the annual rural fairs. Many shops are set up for crowds who come from distant places as well. More often relatives and families meet during these significant occasions annually. Fairs have various categories of small temporary shops and they are punctuated with many snack shops of the local flavours and tastes. A merry-go-round and a giant wheel would always entertain kids and youth among many other attractions such as an instant photo booth, magic show, circus show and film show and even a 'well of death' or a motorcycle 'globe of death' where speeding motorcycles would cross paths.

Even Mumbai is not spared from the fever of the fair. The Mount Mary fair in Bandra in September is a famous one, where crowds from various places would throng the place. In addition to its religious fervour, the whole place would reverberate with many street shops selling all kinds of merchandise. Shopping, eating out and buying souvenirs during that time would be a good deal of fun!

A shandy market is very similar to what is referred to as a flea market globally, which originated in the 1800s in developed economies. Shandy market retailing takes place as large crowds of people visit this open-air market under shacks temporarily erected for the purpose. The shandy markets also provide a platform for many rural entrepreneurs to explore their retailing skills and grow and expand their business. The flea market in developed economies sets itself as a different format from such a street market, as it follows self-imposed governance and code of conduct such as controlled zoning and pricing discipline among the vendors. The flea market has now found place in modern retailing across the world. Such flea markets may soon become an organized format in India too. One may even see flea markets in malls as we are already witnessing their existence in the atria of many malls during festivals in India!

The Traditional Tactics of Retailers to Woo Customers

Here is an old popular Indian grocer story:

> Once upon a time there were two grocers. One was perceived to be good and the other was considered bad. The good one always used to weigh his cereals, pulses, grams, etc. in such a way that if he had to weigh a kilogram he would initially place less than a kilogram in the weighing balance produce and then keep adding to it until it reached the required weight. The bad retailer, on the other hand, always rather unconsciously placed much more and then kept removing stuff from the scales until it weighed a kilogram. The good retailer had actually acquired such skills to create a positive image in the minds of the customers!

The tactic followed, by experience, to obtain the psychological customer loyalty is truly amazing!

I remember the days when my mom used to prepare a list of things to buy for the household every month to stock up and leave it with the grocer to keep ready for my dad to pick it up on his way back from work. While reconciling the bill with the stocks, I recollect (almost two score years ago), once dad found an unbilled pack of dates in the grocery and he quickly went back to return it

A Good Grocer

and the grocer said that it was a freebie for buying grocery worth more than ₹50 in the store! That was the store's way of ensuring customer loyalty those days!

The consumption patterns are changing fast with the way retailers evolve their strategies and tactics as well. They have been changing fast with the way 'urban consumables' are sampled for consumption in smaller versions (but not stripped versions, mind you) with our rural brethren! The inauspicious retailing season of the 'Aadi', 'Ashada' or 'Shravan' month falling between July and August in India, when customer offtakes are at the lowest, has been transformed into a successful selling period, hitting upon the strategy of clearance sales! Result-oriented activations of sales on non-selling times have proved to be true game changers.

The Hearty Service Excellence of Muthulakshmi Stores

A small neighbourhood shopkeeper demonstrates personal touch by being very close to his customers resulting from a genuine concern for them. I have even seen mothers shopping with their small children in his shop often. On one occasion, I witnessed the owner of Muthulakshmi Stores, in my native town of Palayamkottai in Tirunelveli District in Tamil Nadu, offering a crying child of a customer, a hard-boiled sweet free of cost to comfort the child. I have also come across another incident where a busy mother with her uniform-clad son, who too was in a hurry to leave for school, was purchasing a few items from the shop in a hurry and among them she was buying oil to put on her son's hair to dress him up for school. As the mother was busy, the shopkeeper himself applied the small quantity of oil she had purchased on her son's head and combed his hair too. What an amazing help it was for the busy mother! And who other than a neighbourhood shopkeeper can offer it with such a personal touch? The genuine service of small retailers comes from their hearts!

Stretching Beyond Limits to Serve Customers

The very fabric of Indian traditional retailing is different. Recently, I had two experiences when I visited Chennai. One, as a petty shopkeeper in the Velachery area was closing the shop for the day, I rushed to the store asking for a beverage can and the storeowner did not want to disappoint me. He switched on the lights, served me and then downed his shutters. I could understand that the sale of every stock keeping unit (SKU) in his store was important to him. The need to grab a drink on the go from a petty shop as one walks through the narrow streets in any Indian city is never going to vanish, and as long as these needs drive people to stretch out their arms to the petty shops, they will thrive well, come what may. As for the other, as I was observing shopping in two medium-sized fresh vegetables and fruits stores in Chennai, I was amazed to see the zest and zeal of the customers who were vying with each other to fill their shopping baskets. The two stores I was observing (and purchasing from as well) were very well organized and supported by extremely customer-friendly staff. The product mix ranged from mangoes to mangosteen! The prices too were very reasonable. In a country like ours, managing wide and deep assortments of multiple fresh categories is a humongous task. How on earth is anyone going to understand easily the game of the ever-changing diversity of localized customer offtake and the dynamic 'basket behaviour' of a typical Indian housewife without the help of our own native retailers?

Our native small retailers cannot continue to operate the retail business the same way they have been doing for the last so many years. They need to take stock of the situation, the environment, the constraints, the strengths and the opportunities and chalk out relevant strategies to win customers on a larger scale and expand the business. The result of winning in a single store environment has to be extended and expanded to operate in a multiple store environment. Modern or traditional, it is only the entrepreneurial passion that brings a retailer closer to customers!

The Significance of Micro, Small and Medium Enterprise (MSME) Retailing in India

CHAPTER 2

> *The market in India is huge with its consuming population and this ensures the growth of retail businesses.*

In India, the Micro, Small and Medium Enterprises (MSME), also known as 'town and village enterprises' in the manufacturing and service sectors, have been considered to be quite significant in their contribution to the GDP growth of the country. The Micro, Small and Medium Enterprises Development Act (MSMED Act) was enacted in India in 2006, and it facilitates the promotion of MSMEs in India. The act embraces any commercial activity permissible under law, that is, any type of manufacturing, processing or industrial activity or trading or allied operations to fall under the MSME category. Besides manufacturing, a plethora of service activities such as medical/legal transcription activities, call centres, event development and animation, video, filmmaking, marketing consultancy, equipment rental and leasing, laundry, X-rays/pathology, tailoring, studios and cable TV network get due benefits consequent to the categorization as MSME in India. For a common understanding of the enterprises, the following classification parameters are provided in the act to differentiate and define each category of enterprise:

Enterprise	Manufacturing (Investment in Plant & Machinery)	Services (Investment in Equipment)
Micro Enterprise	Does not exceed ₹2.5 million	Does not exceed ₹1 million
Small Enterprise	More than ₹2.5 million but does not exceed ₹50 million	More than ₹1 million but does not exceed ₹20 million
Medium Enterprise	More than ₹50 million but does not exceed ₹100 million	More than ₹20 million but does not exceed ₹50 million

Source: http://www.dcmsme.gov.in/ssiindia

Banks offer assistance to the growth of MSME in India. Further, banks came up with specific policies to fund and facilitate MSME through single window dispensation, quick decision with least turnaround time through specially constituted MSME cells and, above all, banks prioritized cluster based schemes for funding MSME with better service. When it comes to the retail sector, micro, small and medium retailers have not been mentioned in the Act in specific. But it is assumed that the same parameters as applicable for MSME mentioned in the foregoing table under services are applicable for retailers also.

It's time retailers organized themselves as MSME retailers to gain from the consumer revolution that is happening currently. The small- and medium-sized retailers in India must look at the burgeoning internal consumption that is taking place in India. The growing middle class of consumers with enlightened awareness levels can form a captive customer base for all our retail stores in India. The awareness created by media, which has proliferated into the smallest households in India, has augmented the Indian consumers' knowledge and awareness levels. New lifestyles have been a part of the lives of average Indians of late. The increase in the number of working women has been significant and this is causing a good deal of demand for packaged and ready-to-eat foods in India. Even in the smallest villages and towns of India, we see great infrastructure developments that can accommodate multiple shop premises in a market cluster. Infrastructure developments such as the expressways and highways have helped in faster transportation of goods and services across the country in shorter cycle times. Supply chain improvements have taken place as our country is now well networked by roads, railways and airways. Cold chains are being set up with government subsidies in each state and this actually helps control the wastage of food and grains. The market in India is huge with its consuming population and this is the right time to see that retail businesses grow. Small and medium traditional retailers need not vanish if proper steps are taken to strengthen the business.

> One has to think about organizing the business in every possible way to make it attractive for the owner's next generation to take over and proudly run the business.

The thought that the small retail business could see its end with the father's generation should be erased completely from the minds of the present younger generation. One has to think about organizing the business in every possible way to make it attractive for the son's/daughter's generation to take over and proudly run the business. All these days, the small and medium retailers of India have been the channel and medium vehicle responsible for the promotion of many multinational and domestic FMCG brands. They have even traded off their own store name spaces pushing them into insignificance in order to give way for large signages of the brands that they have been selling.

James Gulliver, the son of a grocer in Campbeltown, Scotland, became the chairman of Argyll group, one of Britain's most popular food retailing businesses. Earlier Gulliver joined Fine Fare, a supermarket chain in Britain in 1965 in customer relations, and he soon worked his way to become its managing director. He spared no pains to turn the company around into a profitable one between 1967 and 1972. The key learning, according to him, that resulted in profits was the sheer attention to every detail of the business and then he coined the popular retail adage, '*Retail is Detail*'. Yes, every detail in retailing is important—details relating to the entire environment retail operates in. The elements in the retail environment are the following:

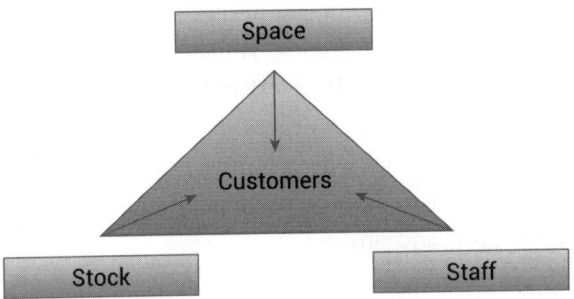

Details of every aspect pertaining to customers are: who the store's customers are, where they come from, what they want, when they need what, how they buy, etc. Likewise, the details of space relate to: how much space is rent paid for, what is the rent per square foot, how much is the retailing space/staff movement space/storage area, how is the utilization of space with reference to stock per square foot, how much is the sales per square foot in a month and how much shelving space is created and used, etc. The details of stock refer to: what stocks in what quantities, in what mix and assortment, in what time periods, in what margins and prices and from which sources. The staff details are: how many sales and delivery people should be employed to serve how many customers and how much is the sales value per person per day, etc.

All these details ought to be looked into without fail to achieve store profitability. A small and medium retail store cannot look at all these details with the help of a shop manual or by dint of only practical experience, but it may have to look into the actual details by ensuring the application of proper systems as the business grows.

The small- and medium-sized retailers whose sales turnover is less than ₹2 million per annum do not have to register under GST in India. Items that are sold in retail stores in lose as commodities are also spared from the GST net. This helps small retailers focus on their sales and customers. Though these exemptions would favour small retailers, it is an astonishing fact that many of them do not have bank accounts yet. The Government of India is focused on bringing about growth in the MSME sector, and in its 2018–2019 fiscal budget, the finance minister announced a reduction in corporate tax to 25 per cent from 30 per cent for companies with a turnover up to ₹2.5 billion. Such changes amounting to savings would undoubtedly help retailers in this sector grow and prosper.

Organizing the Small Store for Growth_The Somanur Grocery Store

Somanur *Maligai Kadai* (in Tamil) was first opened in Erode in Tamil Nadu as a very small kirana store by Mr T. Thanushgaran, founder of Kannan Department Store, Coimbatore (see case illustration in Secret 10). Mr Thanushgaran took the first step to organize his business by opening a bank account. He began to bill products to customers and keep his books of accounts clear. He says that it is by this practice, though any law did not require him to begin these organized practices then, he could really grow. The first point that he mentions is that the bank came forward to fund him, as his business was very organized. So, from a small shop he could grow into a big chain of retail shops soon. Here is a big lesson to the many small- and medium-sized retailers of India, who also can grow big if only they organize their business. Necessary funds can be availed as loan from banks based on their business turnover. These stores can avail of term loans and running cash credits. Many small retailers who would otherwise seek personal, unsecured loans at unreasonable interest, can organize their business well and emerge as successful ones.

Phoenix Mall, Lower Parel, Mumbai

The textile manufacturing business dwindled with time after going through its revolution in the early 1970s. Many in Mumbai's Parel area, which was once the hub of textile manufacturing, did not know what to do and let the mill properties go dilapidated with time. One man had the vision to work on his wasteland and it was time to realize returns by deploying the old factory space for retailing. He worked on it and hit upon the idea of creating an entertainment centre first in 1999. The old mill premises soon had a bowling alley when the sport was very new to Indian customers. The game was introduced to many neighbouring offices as a corporate sport to see that footfalls were maintained, much like the five-a-side football game that was introduced a score years ago to companies in Bengaluru for conducting intercompany tournaments during weekends. The first anchor store in the old mill premises was McDonald's, which renovated part of the space for its restaurant with the old towering factory chimney intact, rendering it a big kitchen look! Then the opening of Big Bazaar followed and the mill was turned successfully to a mall! When the state-of-the-art mall by name Crossroads opened at that time in the neighbourhood, many in the industry opined that the death knell has tolled for the mill premises and its desire to become a successful mall has ended as a far-fetched dream. Perseverance paid at the end of it all. Yes, it's the Phoenix Mill at Lower Parel, and the man responsible for raising it from the ashes is Atul Ruia.

Phoenix inherently had a lot of inadequacies though. The location was considered a low profile one which only allowed narrow access to the new mill-turned-mall. There were no takers initially until a few more anchor stores bargained their own de-risking by taking up space in the mall space, facing the main Tulsi Pipe Road so that even if the mall would fail, these stores may have their captive footfalls from the high street side. The mall began to 'rock' and space utilization became very efficient as days went by. The extended part of the mall is appropriately targeted as a premium and luxury retail mix, christened 'Palladium'. The Phoenix mill at Parel did not only emerge as a mall but it also proved to be a successful model for scaling up with its progressively extended formats. Today, the Phoenix Market City mall and its Palladium are big brands to recon with, in the industry characterized by its multilocational rollout.

The Diversity of Indian Consumers and Consumption

CHAPTER 3

> *The consumption story in India is big. The successful retailer is one who understands the diverse tastes and preferences of customers and satisfies their needs and wants.*

Indian consumers' tastes and preferences are diverse, and they can be categorized under a few segments based on what they usually seek.

Heterogeneous Consumption Pattern

So wide is the heterogeneity of tastes in India and so strong is customers' propensity to remain in the taste roots they have grown up from, that it has become very difficult for any modern marketer to understand their needs and wants clearly. For example, there are more than 100 tastes of 'sambar' preferred by various groups of customers in and around the southern states of India. It becomes very difficult to market a brand of 'sambar' powder with a singular taste. Localization in food preferences is so strong that only native retailers have been able to understand customer tastes and preferences easily. Others try a homogeneous mix of products for every store like the huge hyper and supermarkets in Western countries and try to make success of them and eventually fail. It's high time we followed a typical Indian model of food merchandising—one that is decentralized to be located at the unit level as a store-level merchandising initiative. That can work well to achieve profitability rather than following a central planning and replenishment model of merchandising followed by retailers with similar merchandise mix in all the stores across the country as in the Western markets of homogeneous tastes and preferences.

Amazing merchandise localization

The Unique Consumer Segments of India

Mr Kishore Biyani in his book *It Happened in India* defines the unique customer segments of India as India 1, India 2 and India 3—India 1 is the consuming class, India 2 is the serving class and India 3 is the suffering class. He invites attention to the consumption story of India, which, he says, has to be seen from a social perspective. India 2 consists of the people who contribute to the service economy of India and these are the people who serve the rich and consuming population who are India 1. The number of people who serve every average rich household or employer comprise many families. The India 1, India 2 and India 3 construct

Chapter 3 • The Diversity of Indian Consumers and Consumption

may be taken further to map the geographic customer segments of India—the metro, the urban and the rural. So, going forward, we have India 1, India 2 and India 3, each for metro, urban and rural customers.

As retailers may move towards the urban and rural India in future, such mapped classification may become handy to understand consumers and their consumption in greater detail.

> Localization in food preferences is so strong that only native retailers have been able to understand customer tastes and preferences easily.

Hailing from any background of the consumption economies defined earlier, every customer in India seeks the following kinds of satisfaction attributes on any purchase made:

- Attention
- Pleasure
- Convenience
- Value
- Support

Attention: The attention that a consumer may seek may be of various varieties. One common kind of attention an average serving class consumer would seek is by proudly sharing with and showing the neighbour the great merchandise or the bargains he/she has managed to get! Customers often flaunt or show their purchases to their friends and neighbours just to seek their attention and acknowledgement on the merit of the purchase made. Mobile phones and apparel are shown off more than anything else by the present day's youth among their friends. Women would share their bargains more with their neighbours and friends. The rich may show off their latest acquisitions among their peers. Every customer irrespective of any class or segment seeks attention.

Pleasure: Pleasure like attention is common among customers and is sought from every purchase made. The use of a product may result in the making of good food for the palate, or the attire the consumer uses gives him the style he wants to flaunt and that gives him great pleasure. Likewise, the use of every product in some sense or the other may offer a pleasurable experience to the customer.

Convenience: Indian consumers are not great planners and they never do big stock-up buying. They seek convenience to access stores and buy products and services as and when they want. Convenience is the attribute that comes at the top of the mind for a workingwoman as she runs her young family. She seeks easy-to-cook and ready-to-serve products often in order to save time. Also, convenience is about the convenient time of purchasing from stores that are conveniently located as well.

Value: This is a key attribute that every Indian consumer seeks. Value for money is not about buying cheap or economical products and services. But it is about getting the right value for the money spent, say, even on luxury products. Value is something that is more associated with nil wastage of money than with buying more for less. Consumers are proud to get the full value for the money spent on any product or service in terms of the satisfaction obtained.

Support: Customers would always want support at times of need from all the stakeholders of the product or service bought irrespective of the status in the channel—manufacturer, dealer, retailer or whoever. They seek support more from the last-mile-channel participant who is the retailer. When a customer faces a problem with a product or service, he seeks support for proper restoration or replacement.

While it may not be easy for foreign retailers or big retailers to understand local consumer tastes and preferences, it may be easy for the small retailer who is based in the location for long to do so. On the other hand, the local small and medium retailers also have to keep track of changing consumer tastes as newly introduced products often may induce such fresh tastes in customers. So, it is worthwhile to stock relevant new products in order to satisfy fresh customer needs. For example, a few manufacturers now brand the oats meal, which was hitherto considered a diet meal for the sick and it is sold as a breakfast snack. This may be a new need for some health-conscious customers and, hence, even local retailers could stock such products and create demand.

The Indian Consumption Story

Tracking the Indian consumption story from various sources of information, one finds that there is a substantial change that keeps happening in the patterns of consumption. The following are the promising facts about Indian domestic consumption that has been increasing over the years steadily:

- Reduction of poverty will bring down the destitute population in India rapidly and the standard of living for the majority of India's population will keep rising.
- The patterns of Indian consumer spend will keep evolving to move from expenditure on basic needs to discretionary spending which means that expenditure on basic necessities such as food and apparel will decline and discretionary categories such as beauty, hospitality and eating out, communications and health care will increase in larger measures.

So, what would be the implications for the growth of the retail businesses in India?

- These changes in consumption patterns would create newer opportunities for companies.

- Since the middle-class population is the burgeoning sector in India, companies that can offer products and services to meet their needs and wants would find it easier to grow in greater degrees.
- Such businesses that would keep price points low to meet the affordability of consumers can flourish. Various examples of companies offering low price-point products to consumers can be cited, like Unilever who markets and sells low-cost, single-use packets of products such as shampoo, soap and ketchup in order to make its products affordable for lower income consumers in the rural and urban areas of India who often shop daily for their necessities. Naturals, the number one unisex beauty salon offering its customers hair and beauty care in low price points, has spread its wings even in small towns across India. Instant masala companies such as Aachi Masala, food product companies such as Haldiram's and biscuit marketers such as Britannia and Parle also have small packets for one-time consumption at single-digit rupee price points.
- Companies that can offer products and services to meet the natural, organic and herbal needs of Indian customers can grow by leaps and bounds. Patanjali is a big example of a brand that has not only created a niche in this area, but it also has created for itself multitudes of brand loyal customers.

As the television made inroads into rural homes that carried messages and information about products to the deepest corners of India, likewise, the social media is making a big difference in the lives of Indians at large. The social media penetration is very high, which enables customers in remote places also to know about products and services instantly so that they can buy and enjoy. These are the unique transformations that have been changing the consumption patterns in India leading to the big growth in internal consumption.

The Domestic Merchandising Model of Westside

Propelled by internal consumption, Indian retailing never fails to tap the potential of the growing youth segment. Here's an example of Tata's Westside. Sensing a tough competition in the department store format space in Indian modern retailing with the likes of Shoppers Stop and Lifestyle, Tata's Westside wanted to be different. In 1998, Tata's Trent was established as part of the Tata Group and subsequently the company opened its first store in Hughes Road, in South Mumbai. Although there was no competition in the location, Westside felt the need to be different to emerge successful. Under the retail umbrella of Trent Limited, there are three retail brand stores—Westside, Star Bazaar and Landmark. Westside is a department store format in a floor plate size span ranging from 8,000 to 5,000 square feet. Star Bazaar, established in 2004, is a hypermarket format spread in a large expanse of space with merchandise ranging from in-house apparel for all, accessories to food and grocery products and consumer electronics to household appliances at low prices. Landmark, formerly a Chennai-based bookstore brand, was acquired by Trent in 2005, which currently stocks curios, books and other gift/entertainment merchandise.

The core of our discussion is the distinct differentiation of Westside as a store format from its competitors. Trent has close to 85 Westside stores spread across the country—many housed as anchors in the various malls of India and some established as freestanding stores—the likes of the ones in Hughes Road, Kalaghoda, etc. The quick differentiation of Westside as compared to its other immediate competitors—Shoppers Stop and Lifestyle, results from the store's distinct merchandise strategy rendering it as clear product differentiation. While the competition is about selling various popular brands under one roof, Westside's strategy is to sell its own private label brands targeted towards the trendy youth. The competition carries only 30 per cent of its private labels, whereas Westside carries its own merchandise, styled and perfected thoroughly, in-house. In a growing market where value is of prime concern for customers, it has been a challenge for retailers to offer value while retaining a good gross margin. Even small retailers in the food and grocery sector in India, as we are aware, have adopted the strategy of breaking commodity bulk, packing each product variety and labelling their own way to offer customers the same quality that national and international brands would offer, but at a much lower price. Likewise, Westside saw a huge opportunity for selling private labels in the apparel fashion sector. The company focused on a skilful merchandising team that put together a good range of merchandise in categories such as men's, women's, kids', home and beauty and bath. Style and fashion have been the focus of the designers of merchandise in the organization. The merchandising and buying teams have identified the right suppliers for the designs made by the company merchandisers and every detail is being looked into with the deepest concentration for sustaining quality and currency of styles as part of the company's continuous quality improvement process.

Westside has successfully created private brands such as Ascot, Weststreet, Westsport, NUON, Oak and Keel, ETA and Westsport Active in the men's category and brands such as Bombay Paisley, Gia, Love, Utsa, Mix n Match, NUON, Vark Kurtas, Sassisoda, Zuba, Intima and Westsport Active in the women's category. Studio West comprises the store's products in the areas of bath and body, cosmetics and fragrances. The kids' section carries the carefully curated brands of Baby Hop, Hop and Young and Free that explain themselves with reference to the age groups of the kids. The company took a few years in the initial stage of its growth to make customers buy its own brands. Where national and international brands have clear consumer pull, as a result of their already known brand status, Westside puts in its efforts to build style, fashion and quality in all its domestically developed products to lure customers. Westside targeted the youth with differentiated styles and they have become the core customers for

Westside. It is said that the competitors' profiles of customers are a cut older than those of Westside. Such has been the communication of Westside that the organization modelled very trendy youthful merchandise accompanied by the right visuals. In the matter of pricing, Westside merchandise styles are very economically priced—almost 30 per cent to 40 per cent less as compared to the popular national and international brands. But their merchandise lines match the currency of fashion and quality by all means and, hence, the store brand has been successful. Since the complete focus in on building merchandise around all the in-store brands, the organization is said to have a robust bottom-line which supports its organic growth and its expansion.

Club West is the loyalty programme of Westside and every customer shopping in Westside is a member of this loyalty initiative that is successfully run. Club West customers are given the opportunity to earn and burn points. Club West Classic and Club West Gold are the levels of customer memberships awarded based on the accrued quantum of purchase, and the membership offers loyal customers, significant points to earn. The membership is linked to its additional format Landmark as well. All these strategies put together make the Westside brand distinctly different from its competitors and make it emerge as a successful one in the Indian retail sector.

Factors Fuelling Retail Growth in India

CHAPTER 4

[*Small retailers have the advantage of wielding great penetration power to establish in smaller catchments and grow.*]

Many factors are responsible for the growth of retailing in India. Currently, the consumer profiles are upgrading by themselves as they are increasingly exposed to newer means and varieties of consumption. Increase in consumption is one of the key factors that contribute to the growth of retailing in India. The sheer extension of cities and towns with the creation of new colonies and customer catchments has also triggered the need for more retail stores across the country. Where big retailers cannot penetrate, small retailers have been busy opening stores in new catchments. The following are some of the key factors responsible for the growth of retailing in India, which need to be borne in mind by every retailer:

Consuming Population: The big population of India that was once considered a big disadvantage has become a huge plus point for our economy now. The Indian economy grows because of the domestic internal consumption that is now estimated at more than 630 billion US dollars a year. The growth in population and its growing income levels are a cause for achieving greater levels of consumption in India. The middle class of India is a burgeoning segment and India's spending middle class is estimated at more than 250 million currently. McKinsey Global Institute forecasts that India's total household consumption is expected to multiply four times in just two decades, between 2005 and 2025. It also estimates that the country's middle class will be 583 million strong by 2025, making India the world's fifth-largest consumer market.

Communication: The growth of consumption in the innermost parts of rural India is a consequence of information dissemination on various lifestyles and communication by the media. While telecom has networked the whole of India, movies and cricket have made the youth of India vibrant and brimming with energy to emulate the stars! Facebook has seen many from across India network socially with passion in their very own vernacular expressions! Communication has helped in making every consumer aware about products and services. The media, especially the every-home-access television, has played a major role in augmenting consumer awareness by carrying messages and information about products and services to even the remotest rural corners of India.

Product Proliferation: Many companies have introduced new products as new organizations themselves have sprung up in India. New brands of masalas, oils and FMCG products such as soaps, toothpastes and other body care products and snack food products have been increasingly introduced in India, and these are being consumed by India's mass population. In the last two decades, large national FMCG companies such as ITC, Godrej, Hindustan Unilever, Procter & Gamble, Colgate Palmolive, Cadbury, Britannia, Dabur, Patanjali and Haldiram's and regional companies such as Hatsun Foods, Double Horse, Aachi Masala, Eastern Masala, CavinKare, Sakthi Masala and Lion Dates have established their products in a big way in the marketplace in their respective states. The sheer increase in the product and brand range in terms of width has been helping both consumers and retailers gain momentum in both consumption and sales respectively.

Infrastructure: The building of roads, highways and expressways along with the fast development of rail and airways network has resulted in achieving shorter supply chain cycles. The new real estate infrastructure created for retail in many locations has enabled not only retailers but also brands to expand their business in India. The sheer expansion of a city or town is witnessing the creation of new shopping areas and destinations. Around every city's outer ring roads, we find the establishment of new shops. Consumption growth is fuelled by the expansion of the retail business itself. The future scenario may be one where the real estate building shop and store premises will collaborate with retailers to share revenues on performance rather than retailers paying a flat rent every month. Many organizations have built efficient blast freeze cold chains that play a major role in reducing food wastage in India. Farmers and food manufacturers can access these cold storages now at minimum expenses. The Government of India has subsidized with sops the establishment of the cold storage infrastructure across India.

> Technology applications are fast becoming a must to operate retail stores, as it has in the case of the operations of banks and ATMs in India.

IT and Internet Adoption: The trends and patterns are seen changing towards convenient shopping on the Internet, especially by the youth. This is evident from the new direction of business that Homeshop 18, Naaptol, Telebuy, etc. have taken—from being a television-shopping network to a completely transformed e-commerce business. Many e-commerce sites and applications have been launched, and they are being established fast as online retail businesses. Technology developments have been enabling the growth of retailing in India. The new generation retailers use IT applications to achieve business and operating efficiencies. Investments in IT have been made very affordable even for small retailers as IT services are now offered on a monthly subscription basis by the use of cloud by service providers. Simple point-of-sale (POS) applications are now available for deployment at very affordable monthly subscription rates like ₹600 per month and this is a boon for the development of small- and medium-sized retailers in India. Technology applications are fast becoming a must to operate retail stores, as it has in the case of the operations of banks and ATMs in India. Newer applications in the form of 'apps' enable digital marketing in a big way that amounts to cost-efficient communication through smart phones, tablets and computers.

A few e-commerce organizations are successful in India, and marketplace players such as Amazon and Flipkart are said to clinch more than 100,000 sales transactions per day while brick-and-mortar retailers are trying to spruce up their multichannel initiatives. While brick-and-mortar retailers follow a 'wholesale' model where goods are procured from suppliers to sell, pure-play online retailers follow the 'agency' or 'marketplace' model. This model works with hordes of agents putting up their merchandise on commonly agreed terms on commission to the e-retailer, and sales delivery and fulfilment is done directly from the agent's end on behalf of the retailer. This has proved to be a successful model that works. Multichannel sales may work to rake in maximum number of transactions per day to the brick-and mortar retailer. In the scenario of small and medium retailer, direct-to-home delivery can be an additional sales channel.

Chitale Bhandu Mithaiwale, Pune

On the banks of the Krishna River, the Limbgaon is situated in Satara district in Maharashtra. Bhaskar Ganesh Chitale lived with his family of eight members in the village 75 years ago. He had a small farm with cattle, mostly buffalos. He and his family made a living by selling milk that the buffaloes yielded. He was known for selling good quality of milk. As days were going on without any trouble, devastation fell upon the family in 1935 as the buffaloes were attacked and killed by a disease. The family was forced to move out of the village and they relocated to another small village called Bhilawadi in Sangli district again on the banks of river Krishna. Bhaskar Rao Chitale was a pragmatic man. He rebuilt his resources of cattle again in the new location and soon the family was not only self-sufficient, but they also had around 500 litres of milk at their disposal to sell every day. Bhaskar Rao thought of expandable ideas and hit upon milk derivatives such as curd, butter, *khawa* and buttermilk that had more shelf life to sell not only in his own village but also in the nearby locations. It all began at home first and then the milk products were sold in the marketplaces of villages.

His younger son Rajabhau Chitale went to Mumbai to pursue his higher education. He began his business of milk sweets there in a small way with the products that were transported by train to Mumbai by his father. Later after selling sweets in small ways, he opened a shop in Mumbai. But it had to be wound up soon after yet another blow of a failed partnership. His elder son Raghunath battled all odds along with his younger brother Rajabhau initially and they moved over to Pune, where Raghunath too had his education. In 1950, Raghunath Rao Chitale established the first Chitale Bhandu Mithaiwale in the heart of Pune city, on Bajirao road, as a small shop, which is now one of the biggest and largest selling stores in Pune. The second retail store opened at Deccan Gymkhana, under the guidance of Rajabhau Chitale. Inspired by the father Shri Bhaskar Ganesh Chitale, the business has been transformed into the most renowned brand in India's food industry. In 1958, the third son Purushottam Chitale, after his education in dairy technology, came back to Bhilawadi and started a big production facility for their sweets. The Chitale sweets became popular not only in Pune but also across India. All the three sons have put in their efforts to make the father's dream come true.

Rising like the phoenix from ashes every now and then, the Chitales fought all odds to emerge successful. Growing from a small business today with six manufacturing units, it has evolved as a chain of sweet shops in Andhra Pradesh, Gujarat, Madhya Pradesh, Maharashtra, etc., under the name 'Chitale Bhandu Mithaiwale' selling delicacies such as *pheda* and *shrikhand*. Be it a typical Maharashtrian delicacy like *bakarwadi*, or tasty, common delicacies such as gulab jamun and *rasagullas*, the Chitales make them available online to customers not only in Maharashtra but also across India, with the adoption of an omnichannel strategy of direct to consumer sales! Now, the next generation with Shrikrishna Chitale, Rajbhau's son and his kin are leading the business growth, effectively upholding the watchword of quality in their modernized evolution.

CHAPTER 5
The Hurdles That Retailers Face in India

> *If retailers organize themselves by registering under the required legislative framework and permissions, they can have access to secure bank funds for growth.*

Retailers face big challenges in India. Increasing competition and squeezed margins have a big negative impact on sales and store profitability respectively.

Intensive Competition

The competition is increasing as many modern retail stores like supermarkets and department stores come up even in the small towns of India. For the small retailers, even hawkers and direct-to-home vendors and sellers are a huge competition. It is always a game of pricing that the retailer plays to increase his sales. The retailer keeps the prices of all essentials less as the customer may have a comfortable feeling of getting all products at the right prices. Indians love good bargains and they always love to bargain too. Retailers often follow the 'loss-leader' pricing strategy and keep nil margins or even go below cost in very essential staple products such as potatoes, onions and dal to gain the confidence of the customer. But this may result in losses for the store. Pressure to price products at lower margins to thwart competition from nearby stores has driven many retailers out of business in India.

Squeezed Margins and Profitability_A Big Challenge for Retailing in India

The Indian retailer has many challenges to face to finally emerge a winner. Profitability issues hurt the growth of retail stores at every unit level. Margins are squeezed because of competition and restriction on selling prices.

MRP Regime

India is one of the very few countries in the world where the maximum retail price (MRP) protects consumers. Retailers are not allowed to sell over and above the MRP. That gives brands and manufacturers the edge to supply at whatever list price they fix for the retailers. Consequently, there is always a tiff between brands/suppliers/manufacturers and the retailers, where the latter ask for more margins and the former express constraints. Retailers clone brands and suppliers' or manufacturer's products or find alternatives to manufacture on their own as private labels and in-house brands. These give more margins to retailers. Every retailer must have his own repacking, outsourcing or manufacturing facilities depending upon his size for developing own products. These can be in convenient local food and snack categories. Simple grocery can be packed under the store's own label as a first step. Local tie-ups can be made for the outsourced manufacturing of products of local flavour such as snack foods and others which often may contribute more than 10 per cent of the store's merchandise sales if not more. Small retailers who have had a successful growth path have devised strategic product mix that could yield maximum margins. The MRP, on the other hand, helps customers pay the exact price marked on the product which is inclusive of taxes and prevents them, especially the customers in the rural areas, from being duped. The recent ruling of the legal metrology department of India specifies that the MRP be printed on every item with expiry dates on relevant products sold online as well. While some e-commerce companies have already complied with the stipulated regulation, others like Flipkart have asked for more time to ensure that their marketplace vendors are in full compliance.

Scaling Buying Power

Small- and medium-sized retailers lack the scale as most of them operate a single store. Their buying power is low as they buy only smaller quantities from brands and suppliers unlike their modern counterparts who may operate on a corporate scale. Quantity-based purchase schemes offered by brands and large suppliers may be unaffordable for small retailers and, hence, there may be a negative impact on the margins of many products as compared to large retailers. In order to address the problem of scale, it is advisable for about 20 to 30 retailers in the vicinity to join hands and have a common buying system on a co-operative platform. About 30 small- and medium-sized vegetable retailers of Powai in Mumbai have joined hands. By turns, they go every day by dawn in a tempo with the specific orders of each retailer to the big wholesale Agricultural Produce Marketing Committee (APMC) market and to the Dadar wholesale market to buy in bulk at low prices and distribute among themselves and this practice is a commendable one that can be adopted anywhere by small- and medium-sized retailers in a catchment area.

Pressure from National Brands and Manufacturers

The big national FMCG brands are known for their attempts to 'push' products into small and medium retail stores through their trade load offers and quantity purchase schemes. Retailers who yield to such pressures are often thrown out of their merchandise balance causing their own stock turns to suffer a great deal. My Pressure Pump Theory of Merchandise Inflation states that as more pressure is given by pushing stocks with offers and schemes, the more stock-mix balance of a retail store is affected by uneven inflation of pushed stocks, which eventually bursts the merchandising system. The small and medium retailers ought to become smart enough to understand their own merchandise mix carefully and integrate backwards with locally available resources to come together to buy products such as milk and packaged water to sell.

> Funding being a critical need for MSME, the business needs to follow best accounting practices so that banks can fund MSME easily.

Operating Expenses

In addition to the aforementioned challenges, the infrastructure cost for retailing is also high. Monthly rentals are skyrocketing even in small towns as they grow. As roads around towns develop, they get extended in great proportions in all directions. Though every catchment may have many shop premises built, the rental demands from landlords keep going high. Though small- and medium-sized retailers may not incur huge manpower costs (as they may employ more family members and relatives), many are sure to incur big occupancy cost in their operations. The quickly successful retailers are those who own the store premises and do not have to shell out a monthly outgoing chunk of an amount as rent. Having said that, one has to take into consideration notional rent as part of the operating expenses of the store. The retailer would also earn the rental amount if he/she leases it away on rent to someone.

Scarcity of Trained Manpower

The retailing sector in India, whether MSME or big formats, faces the major challenge of availability of trained manpower. Especially in the front-end retail functional area of sales, manpower is scarcely available. Though single-family small retailers depend upon family members to run the store, when the next generation takes up assignments elsewhere, the first generation who started the store faces a huge problem to man the store. This could eventually even force the closure of the store. As large retailers expand, they may poach people from the smaller ones with the assurance of larger salaries. This has started happening in towns and cities where big retailers set up shops. Consequently, the employee cost may go high to retain them and this affects the profitability of MSME a great deal. Mr H. Vasanthakumar, owner of the small format home appliances and electronics retail chain in Tamil Nadu, Vasanth and Co, once put it

> We mould and make salespeople out of miry clay like a potter and make them into fine serving pots over time, and all of a sudden, the big retailers come and snatch them away. We then have to start the process of recruiting people afresh and nurturing them with the relevant retailing skills all over again and again.

The retention of people in small retail stores is going to be more by means of emotional employee engagement and empowerment techniques like offering responsibility with trust to co-manage stores with owners. Employee loyalty could only be achieved by forging good relationships, which large retailers would never be able to offer.

While challenges are many, the aforementioned key issues hamper the growth of retailing in India, and the lack of availability of even bank funding for MSME for various reasons stifles the growth and expansion of the MSME segment. Funding being a critical need for MSME, the business needs to follow best accounting practices so that banks can fund MSME easily.

Shoppers Stop_ Building Internal Economies of Scale for Growth

We have seen the aforementioned external economies that are not very conducive yet, but improving a great deal to favour the growth of retailing. But what is critical for the growth of retail organizations in India is a clear focus on building internal scales of economy that would propel the expansion of the organization further.

Procurement Economies: Efficient procurement and buying of products in a thin margin retail scenario becomes significant for growth and achieving scale. When the growth of the retail organization happens, procurement grows, and when procurement grows in good quantities, the bargaining power of the retailer becomes higher, which results in good margins to sustain growth. When Shoppers Stop (began as a small 3,000 square feet men's store in 1991 in Andheri, Mumbai, which is currently a large department store organization in India) was just a small apparel store, the store management focused on developing their own private labels such as Stop, Kashish, Life, Haute Curry and Vettorio Fratini, with better profit margin in a big way besides bargaining for more margin with national brands as the company grew. The company had set its gross margin growth target every quarter in its initial stages of growth for obtaining the required margins. This growth resulted in the company opening its many branches steadily and obtaining procurement related economies of scale.

Administrative Economies: As the company grew more, it could open its branches in many locations. The store space, following its format character, grew to spread over a large expanse, say of 50,000 square feet, which instantly gave the company power to bargain for less rentals from mall owners. Since each store could occupy such a large space, the store became an anchor for the host by which the mall could attract other tenants. Operational expenses could be contained as more branches opened in many locations. Since a large space was available within the store, the company could work on introducing private labels in more categories and it could also open avenues for new brands to come into the store with an offer of more margins.

Technical Economies: Shoppers Stop took the decision of introducing an enterprise resource planning software system even at an early stage of its growth, by the name JDA, which helped the company process information faster at various levels. This has helped the company make quick decisions based on real-time information and analytics. It also set up its technical expertise in product designing that helped merchandisers develop new lines in their private label range.

Financial Economies: When the finances of the company grew, Shoppers Stop had good bargaining power on the interest rates on their debt funding from banks. During the time when the company got its tranches of investments by the way of private equity, its value grew because the company expanded in many locations in its initial years, which finally helped in obtaining investors' subscription of shares many times over, during the initial public offering.

Internal economies of scale work two ways. While growth helps achieve scale of economies, lower prices and costs push growth upwards. If the balance is maintained in a steady space, a retailer of any size can grow into a large organization.

FDI in Retailing: Is It Threatening?

CHAPTER 6

> *Keeping a close relationship with customers and serving them with increased focus on convenience, affordable price and timely deliveries will ensure a winning platform for retailers.*

When the economic reforms of our country were discussed by the American president who recently tried to suggest that foreign direct investment (FDI) in multi-brand retailing could usher in the next phase of big economic development for India, eyebrows were raised. While many sections of the media reacted, the prime minister's office reacted by tweeting its responses that our economy is better off than what he thought it was, quoting UNCTAD report on how attractive a destination our country is for investments. The angry opposition parties reacted more vehemently and attempted to justify our economic model saying that no financial institution in India has failed unlike the situation in the USA where many have collapsed. The US president had added that FDI in retail would not only create jobs in both countries, but it would help India grow. Every saturated economy is looking at growing economies like India to set up shop soon. At the World Trade Organization (WTO), researchers opine that India may participate more aggressively in the General Agreement on Trade in Services (GATS) negotiations, to obtain the benefit in exchange, to remove external barriers in trade services. Being no more than a small player in the global market for distribution services, it is recommended by economists that India be prepared to contain the current regime of wholesale trading, franchising and commission agents' services. To forge a robust import and export strategy, the country has offered to open up retailing to FDI and initiate reforms in the sector to support such commitments. Investments, both in retail and infrastructure, are the need of the hour in India, and the country will bring investments at the right time to the concerned sectors. FDI in retailing with developmental conditions may bring into existence new alliances and relationships in efficient combination—in a lighter vein, like the innovative combination of the tissue paper roll and the health faucet together, seen only in the Indian washrooms—to satisfy the growing global consumers!

> Will these 'daily visit' customers walk into a Walmart or a Tesco every day in India if at all FDI fully opens up and these organizations would set up shop? The actual purchase patterns and their baskets would easily defy any researcher's attempt to understand them!

Many global retail organizations have a strategic intent to grow internationally by opening up their operations in new economies. Everyone eyes the Indian subcontinent, as FDI in retailing has not yet been allowed in full swing and there is a large opportunity in an economy that is supported by strong internal consumption from a large consumer base. Ticket sizes in India may be small as compared to developed economies, but the repeated consumer visits have been creating multiple ripples on the topline of the retail business. In developed economies, we have heard about 'stock-up' buying and 'top-up' buying, but in the case of India for the majority of customers it is only 'daily' buying. More than 12 million retailers are said to operate in India and in almost 90 per cent of these retail stores, more than 70 per cent of each store's customers visit the store every day for making purchases. Will these 'daily visit' customers walk into a Walmart or a Tesco every day in India, if at all FDI fully opens up and these organizations would set up shop? The actual purchase patterns and their baskets would easily defy any researcher's attempt to understand them!

Current Status of FDI in Retailing in India

The Government of India has allowed 100 per cent FDI in cash and carry wholesale, in single-brand retailing and in multi-brand retailing of processed food products manufactured in India. For other product categories, FDI is allowed up to 51 per cent with a few conditions. This has raised the expectation that foreign retailers would invest in India, which will eventually spur the growth of the country's economy. For quite a few years now, the pros and cons of FDI in retailing in India have been deliberated upon, and with much thought the entire business is now classified largely into *single-brand* and *multi-brand* retailing, and different norms are being applied so that all the stakeholders are benefited in the long run. It is worthy of note that no other country in the world treats retail with such classifications, though we have come across instances of conditions attached to the FDI policy. Recently, the Cabinet amended the retail FDI policy to allow 100 per cent investment in single-brand retailing through the automatic route with relaxed sourcing conditions, which means that no foreign brand intending to enter into the retailing shores of India need permissions filed through the Foreign Investment Promotion Board (FIPB) any longer.

In the case of multi-brand retailing of products other than processed foods manufactured in India, the condition of a minimum investment of USD 100 million, 50 per cent of which ought to be made in the development of back-end infrastructure within a span of five years, would apply. This shows the Indian FDI policy's long-term commitment towards building robust back-end infrastructure facilities for the future, such as warehousing, sourcing and supply chain. The other conditions are minimum sourcing of 30 per cent from India's domestic small industries/artisans and investor status remain for multi-brand retailing, and these can be complied with ultimately in large multi-category and multi-brand retailing. The multi-brand store organizations with FDI can open stores only in cities with a minimum population of 1 million and this is expected to insulate domestic retailers in small towns from the competitive onslaught of foreign retailers. Going ahead, Indian retailing will see many joint ventures and mergers in multi-brand retailing. The Government of India is promoting the retailing of 'Made in India' goods in the country, and in the event of retailing such products, these mandatory rules may not be imposed on them. Opening the retail sector, 100 per cent FDI has been permitted in domestic trading of food products. The hitherto present 'cash and carry' wholesale organizations will be able to extend their formats to set up their retail stores leveraging their existing fruitful joint ventures and partnerships or forging new alliances.

The decision to allow FDI in multi-brand retailing in categories other than processed foods made in India is left with the respective state governments. Questions have already arisen on what would happen if governments changed and consequently if the reversal of the decisions of earlier governments were to be considered! The government of Maharashtra has already come forward to welcome foreign retailers in the retail sector. One must note that for many large retailers, as much as 30 per cent of revenues come from the state of Maharashtra, especially from the cities of Mumbai and Pune. Mumbai, being the commercial capital of India, will be the front runner not only showcasing the next evolutionary phase of modern retailing to the rest of the country but also spurring a big economic boom. The states that are vehemently opposing the FDI proposal are progressive too in seeking to achieve economic growth and they may not like to be far behind in allowing foreign investments in the retail sector in their states. The consumer pressure too will begin to mount in the near future, to make way for the entry of foreign retailers.

Now that FDI in retailing has been notified in the country, it may be here to stay. To continue to oppose it by means of protests and agitations may only defer its implementation in full swing. It is like the nuclear power project at Kudankulam where the commissioning continued moving ahead in full swing to eventually operationalize the project amidst any opposition, stemming from considerations of safety though. Similarly, even if FDI in retailing is allowed by a limited number of states now, the others may follow suit when there is a change in the policy of the concerned state government or when consumer demand mounts! Customers from the state where FDI in retailing is not allowed may cross borders to buy the merchandise multinationals might sell in the neighbouring state, whose economy may soar at the non-retail-FDI state's cost! The MSME of India, our own domestic retailers, feel threatened by FDI in retailing because of the fear that it may take away the MSME customers and bring their business to naught. But if retailers in India keep a close relationship with customers and serve them with increased focus on convenience and timely deliveries, they are sure to win.

Disruptions to Lure Customers

Stores situated in the local markets and high streets feel insulated from the onslaught of the establishment of any foreign retail stores. As FDI has opened up, many expected that small stores in India may have problems and customers might shift to larger stores. But small retailers are safe even if FDI may loom large in front of them as a spectre to finish them off. Small retailers have their own customers to visit them regularly. They locate their shops in close proximity to their customers' homes unlike the multinational big ones who set up their stores in malls or faraway locations and expect customers to come.

Khan Market and Lajpat Nagar Market in New Delhi

These are popular markets in the New Delhi region, known to exist from time immemorial. Customers find it fulfilling and a great fun to shop around in such typically laid-out market shops that range from small variety shops to convenience stores and groceries to beauty salons. It is said that a branded retail watch showroom in its high pomp and glory opened its doors next to an old small wristwatch store in Khan Market with watch repairing facilities a few years ago and within a year of opening, the big branded store had to close down. The store couldn't even recover its monthly rental cost and could not become operationally viable. Such is the power of the small stores in Khan market, and they can fight any odds that might spring up as a result of the establishment of big international stores.

Sector 17, Chandigarh and Linking Road, Bandra, Mumbai

Sector 17, Chandigarh, is an open mall-like market, fully insulated from the competition of any big mall's housing brands and large stores. The specialty of this market is fashion products. Many Indian brands of footwear, denim, clothing, convenience stores, etc. along with international ones are located in this market. It has many restaurants and a big market of local Punjabi clothing and even wedding gowns. A similar shopping market destination for fashion brands and delightful eateries in Mumbai is the Linking road. Linking road is also famous for its pavement footwear stores for girls and young women and the footwear is available at very low price points. The high point of shopping in this footwear market is the delightful pleasure of bargaining and haggling—and finally finding the unique experience of having won a bargain! In addition, Linking Road has many national and international brands, rendering it the enviable concept of the 'horizontal mall' of Mumbai!

Russel Market, Bengaluru and New Market, Kolkata

The Russel Market and the New Market are very similar in structure. They are conglomerates of small shops situated in a well-laid-out corporation complex of shops that house the product categories of groceries to meat, flowers to vegetables, etc. These markets have small shops that sell products as commodities and customers of all profiles frequent them. It is a pleasure for customers to go around these shops, bargain and buy! Everyday requirements of households could be purchased in a fresh condition from the shops in these markets.

The Ranganathan Street, Chennai

This is a unique marketplace in a street in T. Nagar that branches from Usman Road into the Mambalam railway station. This too is an old market consisting of very small shops selling clothes, footwear, vessels and household items, vegetables and fruits and a whole host of products for varied profiles of customers. So, crowded the street usually is that everyone has to 'rub shoulders' against each other as they move into this street. This street is the place of origin of the famous Saravana Stores, which have found their big expansion into the various locations of Chennai. Low price points are a unique pulling factor for this market, which is said to see the highest footfalls in any shopping location in India. The footfalls are said to go as high as half a million on most busy days! The whole street is populated with pop-up hawking in front of their own small stores in addition to the thousands of small hawkers around the area.

Apart from these markets in India, many new locations have been created consequent to the growth of new colonies of habitation and the extension of roads and ring roads. Bengaluru is a big example of the growth of small- and medium-sized retailers across its new locations—beginning from Marathahalli through the ring road and from Hebbal to almost all catchments adorning the flanks of the road till the new international airport. The extensions of towns also have created new locations for small stores selling various categories of products. The result of allowing FDI in retailing has been seen to add to newer retail formats and it is seen to be bringing in additional avenues of shopping for the shoppers of India!

No Threat of 'Burger King' in Pune!

As my friend Ajoy and I were driving in the city of Pune after a morning meeting on a Saturday some years ago, we were wondering if we could have our lunch at the Great Punjab or at Dario's. Not in a mood to sit and dine in a fine dining restaurant, we thought of grabbing some fast food on the go. My friend instantaneously became nostalgic as we were rummaging through more options, and he suggested that we went to Pune's 'Burger King'. While I was keen about knowing more about this place, he continued to tell me how he had enjoyed the various kinds of burgers served at the 'Burger King' in Koregaon Park in Pune. We parked our car as we reached the location and I walked in disbelief wondering where in Pune one ever had a Burger King then (at that time it was not launched in India!). It was a shack that housed the Burger King and it very much resembled one of the 'paratha' shops that adorn the roadsides of Kerala! The outside space around the restaurant was full of parked motorcycles and cars. The entire place was filled with a crowd of very young people. Famished as both of us were, I thought we might just go straight to order for the burgers, sit at a table and start eating. But when we entered the shack, I could see a serpentine queue of youngsters waiting patiently to register their orders at the solitary cash till. We stood in the queue and placed our orders, all of which—burgers, soft drinks and fries including—totalled to a value of ₹280 only. Though the cashier printed a bill, he wrote my friend's name on it and retained it.

Our orders were not delivered for a good half an hour. At a certain point in time while waiting for the burgers to arrive, I thought that our orders were perhaps forgotten and they were serving those that came after us. It was not so. We were waiting for the delivery of our burgers and I could see suppliers just going around with plates of burgers and fries calling out names of customers seeking their acknowledgement shown by the raising of their hands, to find out where they were sitting so that the burgers could be served. As time was passing by fast, all the names called out by the suppliers sounded to me very much like my friend's name only. Finally, our burgers arrived. I was just taken aback to see the sheer large size of the burgers served that were almost twice the size of McDonald's burgers, if not larger! All these king-sized burgers were only for unit prices of ₹70, ₹50 and thereabouts! The painted price list hung up near the store signage was a few years old, and there were only additions of items to it but no changes in prices made at all. That means the prices have remained without an increase for a few years now! The very thought of such constant steadily behaving prices was incredible, although I could understand the true service motive behind running the restaurant and one could easily understand every reason of its success among the youth! Sinking my teeth into the burger I was enjoying every bit of it simultaneously listening to my friend's account of his glorious student days in Pune and his visits to the 'Burger King'.

I knew that it was a truly youthful, spirited Pune-based outlet. As I looked up, I saw the signboard and the 'King' after the 'Burger' was covered and in some more places erased, leaving it just as, 'Burger ...', without the King. I was told that there was a long drawn legal fight between the international Burger King and the Pune 'Burger King' over the usage of the trademark. Though the court ruled that it was infringement and passing off of trademark on the part of the Pune 'Burger King', the owners seemed to have contended that they started the fast food outlet 20 years ago, much before they knew about the real international Burger King! They complied with the verdict and masked the 'King'.

Business went on as usual in the outlet perhaps more briskly than even before with the signage 'Burger ...' everywhere in the premises! It's only good quality and quantity that matter to today's customers who know how to smartly hang around. The consumer connect has been only with the product experienced in the emotionally enveloping conversations punctuated with oft erupting laughter in happiness among themselves and not clearly with the brand 'Burger King'. Pune's 'Burger ...' was all about the young consumers' emotional connect to the place. The consumers seemed to ask, 'After all what's in a name?'!

Hennes & Mauritz (H&M) and Zara in India

No brand can be a threat to the domestic retail business as long as one is able to tune into the minds of the consumers, understanding what, when and how they truly need products and services. So, a foreign retail brand, though may now find it easier to enter the country, but may have to go through the new learning process of understanding native customers.

Among the recent single-brand retail entrants in mega metros, though with their joint venture structures, the Swedish H&M and the Spanish Zara seem to have cracked the code of attracting customers in loads to their stores. These are lowpriced retailers who have been provided with the right support of information and customer understanding by their Indian joint venture partners. While Arvind Lifestyle Brands had partnered with H&M, Tata's Trent joined hands with Inditex whose brand stable has Zara as a principal retail brand among others such as Forever 21. The price points of the fashionable youth-positioned apparel and accessories sold in these brand stores range from even the lowest price point of ₹149 for a T-shirt to a denim trouser sold at an affordable price of ₹699 for ladies and ₹999 for men. The success and the sustainability of the retailers are attributed to the consumer knowledge shared by the domestic store's operating personnel, governed largely by the local JV partners. Such success is more a consequence of the styles and prices than the brand names per se, as these brands have been relatively unknown to Indian mass consumers until they entered the cities of India through successful malls.

Foreign or Indian, Big Retailers Pose the Same Threat

CHAPTER 7

> *Retailers who constantly identify gaps in competition and fill the same in their own original ways while delivering products and services would see stickiness of customers with them.*

The MSME retail segment is not just threatened by the entry of the foreign retailers into our land but they are also threatened in an equal measure, if not more, by the expansion of the big retailers of our own Indian origin such as Big Bazaar, Star Bazaar, Spencer's, More, Reliance Mart and Nilgiri's! The fear is that large retailers will attract all the customers by their product range and price, which may kill the very existence of the MSME segment in India. Some reports say that there are more than 12 million small and medium retailers in India. The fear is genuine whether the threat comes from foreign retailers or the Indian giants. Often new competition can put in the right energies in us to forge ahead and become stronger. The MSME segment in India need not be afraid of the big competition coming from modern retailers as they have the strength that they have not yet explored in themselves.

Even in a scenario where foreign retailers and big retailers are not present in a town, it is only prudent on the part of the small retail segment to become operationally efficient to make profits and expand the size or get into allied new businesses. Such efficiencies would only enable retailers to provide quality service to customers and sell merchandise at competitive prices. India's consumption is huge and yet there is a big scope for small and medium retailers to grow. Gone are the days when small retailers handled only a limited number of SKUs to remember them by heart and reorder by gut feel. Since they now handle many more SKUs as FMCG suppliers are expanding in large numbers with their ever-widening product range in multi-categories, it is only advisable to find a process by which merchandise quantities are managed to have the best yields at optimum levels. Developing capabilities like preparation of localized products and snack manufacturing in a back-end kitchen will help small and medium retailers grow.

Goliath was big enough to be hit by the tiny David easily. Strategies alone need to be worked out well. The sling has to work and hit the target right on the forehead where the gap is! Domestic retailers have to think of the many strategies that they can deploy to successfully compete with foreign or large retailers. If the strategies were new and exciting, the younger generation would not mind taking over the reins of management of the family retail stores.

> A permanent solution to their problems can be found only if they make themselves stronger by increasing their operational, merchandising and customer acquisition/retention capabilities.

Many soft drink brands in India fell by the wayside as Pepsi and Coke started to rule the Indian beverage market because they tried to copy and emulate the big brands. Perhaps if they had stuck to the original 200 ml bottles, many brands such as our native Parnar and Bovonto may not have had a tough time in a state like Tamil Nadu!

Legal protection may not do the trick! The example of opening FDI to multinational retailers in Thailand has mixed lessons for us. When Thailand faced its economic crisis in 1997, retailers found it very difficult to find funds for their expansion. Bank funding became scarce, consequent to the economic turmoil the country was in. Once FDI was allowed, multinational retailers came in with their investments in Thailand. Retailers such as Tesco Lotus, Big C, Makro and 7 Eleven made inroads into the length and breadth of the country with their expansion. Their growth percolated into the upcountry and rural areas of the country as well.

The market that was, thus, once open to foreign investment freely was later threatened by the military-run government's proposed bill to restrict the expansion and the entry of new foreign retailers in 2007 to protect 'small and medium' and 'mom and pop' retailers. The government's ire was also ignited by the high-handed behaviour of multinational retailers who charged a marketing fee for products from suppliers, which impacted the profitability of domestic traders and manufacturers. This impact, in fact, added to the economic woe already caused by the global recession to Thailand's export economy. Large retailers tend to get their commitments from small suppliers by making them pay an 'engagement fee' often, and even in India, we have instances of large retailers charging what they call 'listing fee' for every product-line or category. Although a one-time fee, this adds to the problems of small suppliers and manufacturers. Every time a manufacturer introduces a new product, the listing fee needs to be paid. In India, suppliers of FMCG and national brand marketers will extend their support in various ways to our small- and medium-sized retailers to break the growing bargaining power of large retailers. Large retailers ultimately have to tread carefully as they get into the shores of a new country.

Though the draft bill is still under consideration, the fact remains that small retailers cannot be made stronger by legally restricting the operational activities of the larger retailers. Since the legislation is still under consideration, it may only inhibit the expansion or entry plans of foreign retailers in Thailand. Fearing a negative impact on the country's economy, the government has not yet gone ahead with the implementation of the draft bill to restrict the business activities of multinational retailers. Research has shown that small retailers could lose their competitive teeth if they are protected. Protection may come in the form of restrictive conditions on the expansion of multinational retailers in terms of controlling their zones of expansion and their hours of operation. There may be a temporary respite that could come to small and mom and pop retailers by controlling the growth of multinational retailers and providing a competition-free environment to them. The more policies are implemented to restrain the growth of multinational retailers, the weaker local retailers may become, laden with the inability to compete with large retailers at all. A permanent solution to their problems can be found only if they make themselves stronger by increasing their operational, merchandising and customer acquisition/retention capabilities. Analysts observe that the focus ought to be on making small and mom and pop retailers more competitive by training them and by building management capability in them to analyse business performance professionally and take decisions to improve their business accordingly. They also believe that small retailer transformation and support programmes should be implemented rather than restricting larger retailers who will have the capability to benefit a country's economy by increasing consumption.

While protests against the entry of foreign retailers and the efforts taken to protect small retailers are in progress, seldom have retailers and trade bodies come forward to help them at the ground level to fight any expected onslaughts from competition from larger retailers. Further, many small retailers are under the impression that the large retailers may charge less prices as loss-leader and predatory strategies adopted temporarily with the objective of driving them away from the business initially and later profiteering by charging customers much more. The small retailers must closely work with regional and national brands and collectively seek more margins for growth. Customers would never sympathize with any retailer, small or petty, and they would never buy the same product at higher prices from anyone. They are highly sensitive to prices.

FDI in retailing would actually increase the overall retailing space in India, and many members of the traditional retailing families and their posterity may take up rewarding challenges to fight large retailers with their inherently acquired traditional retailing capabilities! We are good at what we are, and let us strengthen our domestic retailing skills to win over customers rather than trying to emulate the look and feel of large competing retailers for no reason!

Exclusivity and Inclusivity in the Coexistence of Small and Big Retailers

In fact, the onslaught of predatory pricing by online retailers has affected even the large retailers in India in recent times. Many popular online retailers chase their topline revenues without being considerate about the bottom lines. The concept of following online company valuations by the topline and by what is known as gross merchandise value (GMV), which is derived by the sum total of selling values of all the items spread out by the online retailer in their marketplace for sales. So, the focus has been to enlist as many vendors and marketplace partners as possible to clinch maximum sales and by reducing prices drastically. Often the prices of fulfilment supplies made by marketplace vendors are more than the selling prices in the case of many items in many online retail sites. This is a concerted effort to increase revenues and the government has not put any strictures seriously to bring the erring online companies to book. 100 per cent FDI is allowed in online retailing as the business is considered to be business-to-business (B2B) wholesale trade as the online sales company's primary customers are its marketplace partners. But the online sales site becomes a veritable retail medium to sell products and services to final customers. This may affect the brick-and-mortar retailers to a large extent until they manage competition by their own effective pricing and promotional management.

In yesteryears, we witnessed the fall of e-commerce and many websites, established with expectations to make good business sense, failed. They stood by themselves as individual business entities and waged a lone battle. Separate entities were burdened with the management of a completely independent merchandise mix for each retail format. There was a need to hold high inventory levels. It also became an operational handicap for these organizations that finally faced business viability issues. These individually managed entities demanded exclusive warehouses and distribution systems. Separation between online and real retail operations also led to business practices and policies that failed to deliver unified product delivery and service image, ultimately confusing customers. Adding to their woes, laptop penetration was low. We did not have those many gadgets such as tablets and smart phones to use. Many customers were scared of using credit cards on the internet. The business valuation game was played based on a 'build-show-transfer' model where entrepreneurs were motivated to build e-commerce sites with the sole objective of increasing valuation to palm them off at profits. During the days when the economy was growing at breakneck speed in the United States, new online businesses had great valuation-building opportunities. We experienced its rub-off in India too, but for a short while, luckily! Many hard format retailers too established separate e-commerce companies, which were closed later with the same speed at which they opened!

The online 'game' is on again now. E-commerce is back in action. Many e-commerce sites have opened and are said to be doing good business. We see reports of huge funding deployed in many e-commerce organizations. E-commerce business models have changed. The opening of user-friendly websites to book railway and air-tickets gave rise to many first-time users of e-commerce sites in India in a big way in the recent years. The use of technology/applications in computers, laptops, handheld tablets and mobile phones has changed the way people buy. E-commerce organizations support customers with their easy-to-use apps. Secure payment gateways help customers in their confident buying. In other words, customers now have the confidence to use credit cards on the net. Successful e-commerce initiatives currently are the ones not hijacked by quick-buck-minded investors to drive the valuation game alone. They are the ones focused on having a good strategy. They are bottom-line driven to achieve sustainable scale. They cannot fall easily. Redbus.in first wrote the code for the software that would be required to run the operations of the bus operators and they still stay on ground anchored with the base of their operating alliances—a strategy to handhold and grow for a long time to come. Many brick-and-mortar retailers have forgotten standalone e-commerce now. They are now adopting an omnichannel strategy to become successful. Cross-channel optimization is being done in multi-channel retailing as a multi-channel retailing organization has the opportunity to use each one efficiently to promote the other. With reference to developed economies, it is said that 65 per cent to 75 per cent of consumers have researched a product online and purchased that product offline. Of those people, a figure ranging from 50 per cent to 60 per cent are said to have cross-channel shopped in the past. That's happening fast in India too. As online businesses take off, they only need a grounding strategy to integrate with other channels and alliances efficiently to reach customers. All said, this nation of retailers would always see eras of coexistence!

With large retailers around in the cities and towns of India, there emerge new business opportunities for many small retailers. The location where a large departmental store or a hypermarket business or a mall is established becomes a retail zone itself. With stiff competition from online retailers, the whole retail industry has gone through a phase of consolidation, while having become conscious of giving products and services to customers at affordable prices. Large retailers, malls and online retailers compete with each other but they do not affect small retailers in any big way. Small retailers go their unique way of product niche exclusivity, service exclusivity or catchment locational exclusivity to satisfy their customers.

When the Shoppers Stop department store opened in Andheri East in Mumbai, the nearby area became a prominent location for the retail business. The complex situated diagonally opposite Shoppers Stop in that area became a footwear bazaar soon with brand stores such as Bata and Lord's Metro. Small vendors also have their field days, as the whole area becomes one of a *mela* surrounding in the evenings and on weekends. Sellers vending balloons, cotton candy and ice cream throng the place in front of Shoppers Stop every evening.

When I was part of the team of managers running the retail operations of Shoppers Stop, the company headquarters was located on the 4th floor of the department store itself. I used to hear of the interesting instances that happened around the store at different points in time. B. S. Nagesh, the cofounder and vice chairman of Shoppers Stop, was the general manager of the company that was then operating a single small store in 1991. One of the actual stories he narrated, pertained to the development of street vendors around his first store. It was a regular practice in the store to run many events as part of its promotional programmes throughout the year. On certain festival days and promotional campaign days, the store manager used to announce special daily targets for the store with the promise that all the store employees would get to have a cone of ice cream on achieving the target. At the end of the day, the mobile ice cream vendor would arrive at the store early enough, not only being ready with his ice-cream stock (and selling to customers in front of the store as well), but also following up eagerly with employees, encouraging them to achieve the day's target!

Similarly, the place around Phoenix Market City mall in Velachery, Chennai, has become a big marketplace housing many retail stores and eateries throughout the length and breadth of the roads intersecting the mall zone. Large retailers, hypermarkets and malls have not negatively impacted small retailers' sales in a big way. The big retailers and malls have only made their locations and their catchments busy and buzzing with loads of customers for even small retailers to exploit such new opportunities.

The Changing Face of Retail Communication

CHAPTER 8

> *A happy shopping experience can be provided to customers only by communicating and interacting with them with an objective to understand them and win them for a lifetime.*

The power of communication is so high that it can work wonders in retailing. Many customers too like salespeople to talk about products and clarify product features before they buy the products. In the process, sales personnel get to understand the consumer psychology well. Using the flattering technique, for instance, they may use phrases like 'You look slimmer in this dress', when a lady customer tries out a garment, which may elate her ego a great deal and induce her to buy. 'One does not know when we'll have this in our store again. This is the last piece in our current fast selling collection' may further hasten the customer to buy. This may successfully create a sense of scarcity so that the customer may not want to miss an opportunity to buy. The third psychological tool that retailers may use is the technique of 'fulfilling an obligation through reciprocity'. This means that a customer may feel obligated to buy for a 'favour' received from the sales floor personnel or the retailer, in the buying process. For instance, when the salesperson has offered the customer multiple alternatives digging through the stocks for long, the customer may be obligated to spend more time in the store and buy or for that matter, it is commonplace in jewellery stores and saree shops in South India to offer snacks and beverages to customers as they go through the salesperson's product range presentation. The customers may not only become hugely obligated to make a purchase but also are retained in the store for a long time enabling better interactions to browse more options which may lead to larger purchases. Automobile retailers may adopt the ploy of talking about the 'difficulty that they face in holding on to the "old" prices for a long time' that may do the trick with customers often. Traditional retailers understand consumer behaviour like the back of their palms and often better than their modern counterparts. So, every customer interaction may result in the achievement of big sales.

Floor activations are a major part of below-the-line communication in retailing. Realizing the need to clear stocks, stores may immediately put up instant communication of on-the-spot offers. This may include visual communication too with the mannequin adorned with the clearance attire. Walmart is known for floor promotional activations like the popular everyday low price (EDLP) enabling customers to compare prices and shop. Walmart offers low prices and communicates the same through 'feature advertisements' in newspapers that helps the store attract a large number of customers. Walmart's strategy is to be aggressive on prices and cost. Even in this digital age, the company assigns its importance to low price and low cost and communicates through price promotions to its customers. According to Walmart's CEO, Doug McMillon, 'EDLP builds customer trust, both in stores and online. That's especially important in a digital era where there's greater price transparency. To deliver price leadership, we continue to focus on driving everyday low cost (EDLC) through improvements in supply chain, processes and other efficiencies' (Q&A with Doug McMillion, excerpted from *Walmart's Annual Report 2015*, published on Walmart website).

Understanding consumer behavioural insights and patterns can help retailers a great deal in the matter of sustaining a long-term relationship with customers while truly helping them buy. Emerging markets like India have a significant growth in consumption, and consumers in India are from diverse cultures and behaviours. They also show different tastes and preferences. In developed economies, they may show similar purchase behaviours in larger regions, and so, various large consumer clusters can show similar behaviour. But in India, consumer purchasing patterns and behaviours are seen to be very diverse. Marketing and retailing organizations cannot operate with the assumed premise that consumers are the same everywhere. While on the aspect of assumption, I am reminded of a story that writer Bill Bright narrates in one of his articles:

> Understanding consumer behavioural insights and patterns can help retailers a great deal in the matter of sustaining a long-term relationship with customers while truly helping them buy.

> There once was a man who was very fond of the famous general Robert E. Lee. Every day the man would take his four-year-old son for a stroll through a nearby park, which had a statue of the general mounted atop his beautiful horse, Traveler. And as they walked, he would say to his little lad, 'Say good morning to General Lee'. And they would say good morning each time they walked by. As the days and weeks passed, the boy got used to the ritual of waving his chubby hand and saying, 'Good morning, General Lee'. Then one day as they walked past the statue, the boy asked his father, 'Daddy, who is that man riding General Lee?'

In online retailing, sales conversions are supported by 'web cookies' that chase customers, always behind them and reminding them through pop-ups constantly. Even an adamantly browsing customer who resists buying often would be lured into purchases by such repeated reminders. Web cookies play a major role in digital marketing. They are also known as 'http cookies' which get into the web browser when one visits a particular website. Over a period of time that is set by the creator, the code is stored in the user's browser unless he deletes it intentionally. This technology supported reminder effort chases the browser during his other web browsing activities as well. The pop-ups enabled by the stored codes are used to re-target customers and bring them back to the targeted websites. The cache memories in the browser store data such as shopping cart information, user preferences, retaining data previously entered into forms with built-in auto-completing functions and so on. Google Analytics has adopted this technology and uses cookies to capture and store volumes of data. They trace facts of how new and returning customers can interact even with their clients' websites. These cookies are often so populated and numerous, they can even remain in the users' browser over long periods of time—ranging from ten minutes to as long as a few years. They have the capability to extract web behavioural information, polled demographic data (such as gender, age, marital status and other personal data, personal interests and location) and e-commerce history too. Marketers and online retailers use Google Analytics linking it to their websites to obtain useful information and data for an intelligent approach to meaningful/rewarding digital marketing.

Retailers are seen to exploit the explosion and proliferation of media, especially the electronic (television) and the digital media. The reach of such media is quite wide and strong in our country. TV carries through the multifarious channels many programmes of regional and local significance. Similarly, the digital media consists of the growing social media network such as Facebook, Twitter and WhatsApp. Retailers in India, big or small, never fail to create their own pages and write their own blogs as well. Even tiny retailer uses digital media effectively. In the fish market in Powai, Mumbai, there is a string of hawkers selling fresh catch every day. A few enterprising fish hawking ladies have the mobile phone numbers of their regular customers. It is an everyday routine for these hawkers to take nice snaps of their 'visually merchandised' and well-laid-out catch and blast these images to their loyal customers! They make follow-up calls too to trigger their footfall into the market! And that's the extent of today's reach of social media marketing!

According to recent news reports, Hindustan Unilever, the world's third largest consumer product marketing firm, has established its Consumer Insight and Innovation Centre at its Mumbai headquarters recently. The centre will facilitate the study of how consumers shop for FMCG in India. The centre is Unilever's first consumer insight study hub in India and its seventh one in the world. It is reported that the centre will serve several of its group companies with an understanding of how consumers shop in various formats of traditional and modern retail stores. Shopper insights would be provided by the centre to both general stores as well as retail chains. The centre will also simulate retail environments of supermarkets and neighbourhood stores inviting customers to shop the virtual stores. Technical devices are used to track their in-store movements and even the movement of their eyes to map and display spots that attract consumer attention. The centre will help retailers especially the neighbourhood ones to attain product displays and consumer offtake efficiencies based on a scientific purchase behaviour study approach. Based on the centre's insights, the company can advise its retailers on how category growth and margin improvements can be achieved. The group companies of Hindustan Unilever will use the shopper insights and data even to plan product packaging and facings for the future. It is said that virtual reality platforms may be used by the centre to study the patterns of consumer purchases of new products and to study the effect of new in-store promotions. A scientific study of consumer behaviour by retailers can go a long way to help customers buy and increase sales in retail at large! As many of us are aware, Paco Underhill, the author of the popular retailing book, *Why We Buy*, studies consumer behaviour from a spatial perspective too. In India, my friend Biju Dominic of FinalMile studies consumer behaviour from a neurological angle. He says, 'Marketers can use neuromarketing to better measure a consumer's preference, as the verbal response given to the question, "Do you like this product?" may not always be the true answer due to cognitive bias'.

The long and short of such retailing communication surely reiterate the true understanding of consumers and reaching them with timely information!

Creative Visual Communication_ Bata's 'Eyecatcher'

Retailing is the only business whose success is dependent upon customer walk-ins: a business that practically does not go to customers but waits for them to come to its premises. Even in modern online retailing, triggers are sent by emails or links are uploaded in social media to instantaneously lead one into browsing for buying. It has always been a challenging task for many brick-and-mortar retailers and malls in India to attract footfalls as standalone entities. Malls depend largely upon their anchors to bring in the right footfalls into the premises. High streets are laden with their huge passing-by population and stores situated there only have to attract those passing-by to set their feet into the store.

In the olden days, there were no malls in India, nor were there any large modern stores as we find nowadays. It was only in the high streets of cities and towns that retail stores could be found. To attract footfalls into the premises, retail stores used to sport very attractive show windows where product displays were made prominent. A little more than a score years ago, bystanders could be thrilled to see a lady mannequin in the local apparel store moving its hands constantly to welcome customers with a 'namaskar'! A male mannequin that kept sipping a glass of cola also used to accompany it (cola drinking was a fashion statement, scores of years ago!). These mannequins were placed right at the entrance in retail stores in high streets and they attracted everyone's attention and consequently footfalls, too. Innovatively, retailers brought those 'deadly' mannequins live with motorized movements to attract footfalls and customer attention!

Some stores had their show windows dressed thematically, updating them with messages that could have their currency significance, much like the Amul hoardings that everyone wanted to wait and watch. The Bata stores organized signature displays of footwear in floral forms that became the standard across all stores. The displays not only had such signature forms but motifs and props, which befitted the season celebrated, accompanied them. Professional window dressers were given guidelines on visual merchandising along with a supply of the required materials and props so that no finer element of the displays across the stores was missed at any cost. The display windows were punctuated with a huge thematic picture, called 'eyecatcher' which compelled every passer-by to look into the store and reminded customers to enter. The eyecatcher changed with the change of theme, every time tuned perfectly to the currency of the season and it was the cynosure of all eyes. The theme ran around the store in communication through festoons and bunting as well, in a very aesthetic manner.

A few of the new age retail concessionaires in airports, in order to attract the busy passers-by, have digital display screens projected; others in high streets have open, see-through windows and yet a few more have open entrances with just piles of table and nested table displays! The Louis Vuitton store in UB City mall in Bengaluru showcases its grandly done windows often. The recent window décor was a visual treat where the displays were designed by a series of white thematic cut-outs of garments beautifully arrayed to attract every customer passing by! Among the many innovative techniques of inviting customers 'loudly' into the retail store, displays and show windows play a permanent and timeless role. The right visual presentation in retail may not only attract the customers but also make them associate themselves with the store striking their instantaneous belongingness! Innovation in visually appealing to customers to bring them into the store will continue through the ages, but with modern 'eyecatchers' though!

Innovative Customer Connectivity at Starbucks

Starbucks in India (a joint venture between Tata Global Beverages and Starbucks) launched its unique app for customers, which combines mobile payment and customer loyalty. Starbucks in India already has a 'My Starbucks Rewards' loyalty programme and when a customer uses the app to order, stars are added through the app itself without needing to swipe the rewards card. The mobile app has recently included a payment system linked to its loyalty programme. This unique initiative makes Tata Starbucks the pioneering retailer in India to be linked to its customers digitally and offer them a mobile payment option where it automatically accrues reward stars. Customers can order, make payment and earn/redeem loyalty stars through the app. By this app, Tata Starbucks India nestles in the principal company's global digital ecosystem.

The key features of Starbucks India mobile app mobile payment include the following:

Scan to Pay: For customers looking for a fast and convenient way to pay, they can quickly scan the barcode linked to a registered Starbucks Card on the mobile app or simply shake their mobile device with the 'Shake to Pay' feature to activate the pay screen.

Starbucks e-Card: Conveniently pay using the virtual Starbucks Card which can be generated and reloaded directly from their mobile device. Customers also can set up automatic reloads. The mobile app features a complete Starbucks Card management system with card registration feature, balance transfer from one card to another and transactions history.

My Starbucks Rewards: Register for My Starbucks Rewards programme, track rewards history and track stars and redemption benefits all using the mobile app.

Store Locator: An easy way to locate the nearest Starbucks store in India.[1]

Recently, Starbucks launched an innovative conversational ordering system in the United States known as 'My Starbucks Barista'. The company also unveiled a new social gifting feature on WeChat, China's leading mobile social communications service. The Starbucks India mobile app rests on its ever-growing technological innovation platform.

---

[1] See www.starbucks.in

Disruptions and Innovations in Indian Retailing

CHAPTER 9

> [*Technology-supported innovations made even small retailers at least learn the art of connecting with their customers using their smart-phone-enabled social media communication tool such as WhatsApp.*]

The words disruption and innovation are lavishly used in the current business scenario where changes in patterns of consumer behaviour occur fast or where even changes in business models happen. When these words are applied in the business context, they have their specific meanings. While 'disruption' means problems or a disturbance that interrupt an event, activity or process—a word that has a negative connotation—innovation as we all are aware means something new—an idea or an invention—that brings transformational change to give better results and enhanced success. The term 'disruptive innovation' augurs well with its usage in business, which refers to the dictionary meaning, 'an innovation that creates a new market and value network and eventually disrupts an existing market and value network, displacing established market leading firms, products and alliances'.

'Tsunamic' Disruptions

In the recent times, a few disruptions made a big impact on the retail business in India. I call them 'tsunamic' disruptions. The major one was the demonetization resulting in the sudden withdrawal of currency notes of a few denominations overnight in November 2016. Since then, for over six months, the small retailers went out of business. Cash was not available for transactions. They were seen running from pillar to post to find new payment systems so that they did not disappoint customers. A total of 80 per cent of India's retailers are small with shops measuring less than 50 square feet in size. A majority of them run stores that are less than 50 square feet in size! They were totally dependent on cash transactions. For close to a year, the turmoil of transactions remained a big challenge for retailers to win over. The brighter side of demonetization for the retailers was the fact that they began to install electronic data capture or swipe machines in collaboration with banks and credit card companies. They started accepting Paytm payment transfers. The small retailers looked up to banks, opened their accounts, many for the first time. The first step of organization/modernization of very small retailers began with demonetization. Some of them have realized that they can avail bank funding through cash credits and term loans.

The second major 'tsunamic' disruption that impacted and, perhaps, is still impacting the retail trade is the implementation of Goods and Services Tax (GST) with differential tax slabs on various categories of products. The realignment is yet happening in terms of percentages levied, 0 per cent, 5 per cent, 12 per cent, 18 per cent and 28 per cent. The various approved agencies of the Government of India facilitated the adoption of the new GST and the filing of returns. The seamless input tax credits were a boon to retailers as the new GST resulted in the avoidance of 'taxation over taxes' or 'cascading-effect' of the incident taxes the system added to the burden of everyone in the supply chain. State and central taxes applicable such as Service Tax, Octroi and Excise Duty separately caused the cascading. This rendered the supply chain tax heavy and the extra tax paid on the already taxed amount was finally charged to the end consumer. Retailers suffered consequent to lower quantum of purchases from customers as a result of

Chapter 9 • Disruptions and Innovations in Indian Retailing

consequent inflation. GST has become a friendly taxation system making retailers transform themselves into organized entities filing proper GST returns.

The third major disruption that happened in the Indian business scenario is the 'technological invasion' as I call it, which has completely changed the way consumers shopped for their products and services. Companies were waiting for laptop and tab penetration and the Internet adoption but when smart phones made their way into the Indian market at very low prices, when the service providers slashed data charges to bare minimum and when every business organization has introduced its own apps, the way consumers shopped changed completely. Retailers especially the small ones are taking their time to adapt to these new styles of shopping by consumers as products and services are exposed to absolutely transparent pricing. Many retailers are yet flabbergasted and dazzled as technological innovations propelled the growth of online retailing in India. The Indian consumers began to buy books and music online, progressed to make their bus, rail, flight and movie bookings online and now they buy all kinds of products online. They come to brick-and-mortar electric stores, browse models, compare prices and buy them online using their mobile phones. The look and feel are rendered by the brick-and-mortar stores but the benefits of the sales are reaped by online retailers who can afford cheaper prices consequent to their huge saving on infrastructure and other operational costs. This too made even small retailers, at least, learn the art of connecting with their customers using their smart-phone-enabled social media communication tool like WhatsApp.

> Many retailers are yet flabbergasted and dazzled as technological innovations propelled the growth of online retailing in India. The Indian consumers began to buy books and music online, progressed to make their bus, rail, flight and movie bookings online and now they buy all kinds of products online.

The communication on social media changed the way retailers looked at their sales promotions. They have been able to make product shots themselves or even shoot videos on their own and communicate with their customers. Retailers abroad closed many of their stores and consolidated their efforts with a mix of online and brick-and-mortar retail. Payless ShoeSource closed almost 400 stores—Macy's 68, JC Penney 138, Abercrombie & Fitch 60, Guess 60, Radio Shack 550, Sam's Club 63, etc.— according to recent reports as they consolidated themselves. On the other hand, Amazon was seen looking for opportunities to open physical stores in a few markets with a reported acquisition attempt in France. A mix of store formats both online and offline seems to be the trending consequence of the global retail consolidation.

Store Format Innovation

Innovation of experiential retail formats in India seems to be working well. One of the examples is the Decathlon store. Decathlon sports stores are almost 60 in number, spread across most of the cities of India. They are located in malls and as freestanding destination stores alongside highways as well. The specialty of the Decathlon store is its offer of a great customer experience. Customers can check a product by trying it inside the store. Kids can cycle inside or a table tennis player can actually play the game before buying the game's wares. Some stores have a model putting area to check and buy golf gear. The highway format has a huge parking area and the store sports all outdoor adventure merchandise as well. The customers are bound to have a truly enjoyable shopping experience. While the old mundane, mass, commercial stores are struggling to offer the right experience and, hence, facing closure, stores that provide the right shopping experience are seen to flourish in the Indian retail landscape.

Disruptive Innovation in Cabbing in India

When one speaks of disruptive innovation in business, one cannot ignore Uber or Ola, a similar cab business in the Indian market. These brands have been seen to have completely taken over the local conveyance business. In a city like Chennai, people no longer use auto-rickshaws but use only Ola or Uber. The Chennai auto-rickshaws have earned a bad name for themselves and they have been notorious for charging higher fares from time immemorial. But in Mumbai, commuters use local auto-rickshaws along with Ola or Uber. The destruction has not been complete. In Kolkata too, similar to Mumbai, people use yellow cabs as well. They have been true to following the rightly metered pricing. Customers patronize both old and the new depending upon convenience and value. Technological advancements have been seen as disruptive tools innovatively supporting business and retailing is one of them. Business Analytics, Big Data, Small Data, Internet of Things, etc. have been supporting the growth of retailing by offering seamless and result-oriented product, service and consumer connectivity.

Disruptive Innovation in Product Development

Product innovations have been helping the growth of retailing in a big way. 'Vada' is a much popular South Indian snack. But many in the modern days find it difficult to make them at home. A company by the name ID Fresh Foods in Bengaluru began its operations in 2006 by making and selling freshly made 'idli' and 'dosa' batter. The company's vision was to prepare and share healthy batter with the whole world, their customers worldwide, just the way they make the batter at home. The product became a big success because people loved the healthy, preservative-free batter. The company now serves millions of homes across India and the Middle East.

After the success of the batter now, the company focused on its innovation in 'vada' making. A ready batter filled in a squeeze container which, on inverting and squeezing into the vessel full of oil during preparation, forms the automatic shape of the 'vada' with a hole in the centre, as it should be. This makes it very convenient for anyone to make the age-old traditional 'vadas'. The product has become an instant success in the marketplace and it has found space in the shelves of many supermarkets in South India. Such product innovations augment demand in the market and retailers fulfil such demands by stocking and selling these innovations.

Consumer Power and Disruptive Innovation Impacting Retailing

'Jallikattu' is a popular traditional Indian sport in which strong men who have the capability to control overcome the raging bulls. This has been a dangerous sport played in the southern parts of India, especially in Madurai in Tamil Nadu on every 15 January, one day after the Tamil festival of Pongal. The day is devoted to decorating and honouring the cows and bulls that help farmers in the farm. It is also the day when people test their capabilities to overcome the raging bulls in an open area. People have been seen to die and get hurt too in the process of overcoming and controlling the strong bulls. So, the Supreme Court banned this sport a few years ago. In December 2016, crowds and crowds of people joined together in a massive gathering over a fortnight in protest of the ban in the Marina Beach in Chennai. Day by day the gathering gained momentum and the number of people especially the youth, the college students gathering from all over Tamil Nadu became uncontrollably huge. It was a massive protest and finally the Government of India allowed the sport to be played with a reversal of the decision of the Supreme Court. Such is the power of a mass movement. Now look at the products of Patanjali, which has a similar mass consumer movement in its favour. Patanjali with its innovative, natural, healthy and organic product range started giving many global FMCG majors a big run for their money. Healthy, natural and organic products may sweep the minds of consumers and those making and selling these products in retail may become greatly successful. Recent news carries the information of the readiness of one more spiritual guru, Pandit Sri Sri Ravi Shankar, who also plans to open 500 of his retail stores selling products that may be very similar to Patanjali's merchandise sold in their retail stores. Responding to such natural and healthy competition, even the multinational companies have come up with the launch of similar products. Colgate's Vedshakti toothpaste is a relevant example of a recent launch that is targeted to compete with Patanjali's toothpaste 'Dant Kanti'. Such product innovations may centre around good quality, proper pricing, great service and timely fulfilments.

A mass consumer movement may happen in future towards sustainability. It may be a huge sway in favour of recyclable, organic and eco-friendly products. Innovations in these areas would disrupt old products on the shelves and retailers along with consumers would readily adopt them. While process innovations may help manufacturers in big ways, product and service innovations would make huge result-oriented disruptions in retailing in India.

Sri Sri Tattva _ Disruptive Retail Innovation, the Natural, Ayurvedic and Organic Way

Close on the heels of the success of Baba Ramdev's Patanjali stores and sensing a mass movement of consumer preference to natural, organic and ayurvedic products in the future, Spiritual Pandit Sri Sri Ravi Shankar is targeting to roll out 1,000 retail stores by the end of 2018 under the name Sri Sri Tattva, through the franchise route. These stores would sell FMCG and wellness products. Sri Sri Tattva plans to rake in a whopping revenue of ₹5 billion from the retail business in the next 15–18 months. The company has already tied up with Franchise India for the purpose of identifying like-minded franchisees. The store format, quite strikingly similar to Patanjali, is understood to be of three types: Sri Sri Tattva Mart, Sri Sri Tattva Wellness Place and Sri Sri Tattva Home and Health. While the Wellness format may have the advisory services of an ayurvedic doctor, the Home and Health stores are expected to be larger in size, fit to be established in cities and larger towns.

Over the last two years and more, Sri Sri Tattva has been quite aggressively distributing its range of products in the general trade, accessing small- and medium-sized retailers across India. They have also made inroads into modern trade in the recent times. The company's enviable range of products includes dental care, skin and face care, health care and wellness besides nutrition. Sudanta toothpaste and Ojasvita Malt health drink, besides cow's ghee have emerged as Sri Sri Tattva brand's fastest-growing products. In addition, the brand has an array of products and ayurvedic medicines, wide enough to make a large planogram for a freestanding retail store.

Sri Sri Tattva already has a very popularly operational e-commerce website to sell its products online. Groceries and staples, beverages, organics, personal care, health supplements, apparel, home care, incense and fragrances, gifts and even doctor's appointment are significantly promoted on the company's website.

Sri Sri Tattva would sell over 120 of its popular products, comprising 44 products from its personal care range and 82 from the food range on BigBasket, the *Numero Uno* online food and grocery retailer in India, in a collaborative arrangement.

The big disruptive innovation in the market is about the creation of a completely natural and healthy researched productline by companies such as Patanjali and Sri Sri Tattva. They are now able to commercialize their efforts for the benefit of mass consumers in India offering their 'formulas' at affordable prices. The Indian retail market is poised to witness a 'swadeshi' revolution, with both Sri Sri Tattva and Patanjali foraying fast and deep with their retail stores across the country.

CHAPTER 10
India's Rapid Adoption of Online Retailing

[*Retailing in India is going through a new phase of expansion with the adoption of additional models in the online retailing space.*]

The current customer shift is towards the quick adoption of the behaviour of buying goods and services online, thanks to the usage of smart phones for shopping. Retailing products and services using the Internet is fast becoming a common phenomenon worldwide. Companies who have been hitherto retailing through brick-and-mortar stores have begun to use the medium of the Internet as an additional and complementing retail sales channel. Most of them have developed their own apps for enabling customers to shop online in their own comfort and convenience. Almost all the retailing organizations have now put up their products and services for sales online, notwithstanding the format size.

Online Retailing at Walmart

For Walmart, the world's largest retail organization, combining e-commerce with the accessibility of physical stores would create a whole new shopping experience for customers. They can order online and pick up goods from any preferred store; they can shop online and even return goods in any store of the customers' choice. Such is the flexibility and uniqueness of interchannel shopping experience Walmart provides its customers in order to stand out of competition from pure-play online competitors like Amazon. According to a Forbes report, global retailer Walmart's online sales contributes to 3 per cent of its total sales revenue (as of November 2017) and the company expects to grow its domestic online business by a whopping 40 per cent in the fiscal ending 2019. Walmart has devised specific strategies to spread its e-commerce efforts and the company has roped in those experienced especially in the online trade. Walmart is said to have acquired smaller e-commerce companies such as Modcloth, Shoebuy, Moosejaw and Bonobos, which has brought along with them an enviable product portfolio with good margins in the online space. Walmart.com offers ship-to-home, ship-to-store, pick up today, online grocery, as well as transactions through Jet.com. A major part of the company's online sales growth comes by organic means, through Walmart.com, including online grocery that is on a quick growth trajectory. Amazon too is not far behind Walmart in its acquisition efforts in the US, and its recent acquisition of Whole Foods Market has given the company 300 new physical distribution points. Very similar to the online retailing efforts of global retailers, retailers in India too have been adopting online retailing at a rapid pace. In India, we are witnessing the emergence of successful pure-play online retailers too, such as Flipkart, BigBasket and many others.

> Very similar to the online retailing efforts of global retailers, retailers in India too have been adopting online retailing at a rapid pace. In India, we are witnessing the emergence of successful pure-play online retailers too, such as Flipkart, BigBasket and many others.

Online Consumer Behaviour

Online shoppers show a variety of shopping behaviours. One may enjoy window-shopping in a department store or one may love strolling in a mall with the objective of spending time all by oneself or with family for sheer relaxation. Likewise, online customers too enjoy browsing retail sites often, just to understand trends or to know about the latest products or service innovations and introductions. Often while browsing, we are bombarded with information and recommendations continuously based on our browsing history. Even as we open our emails and begin to focus on them, information from various online service providers would pop up distracting our attention, through the cookies stored in cache memory. One is awed many a time about how this tracking machinery could consistently do the job! Offline retailers tend to forget their regular customers, as people's memories are short-lived. Even customer relationship programmes do not have an efficient process to alert the presence of regular customers in the store premises as they seldom deploy any reliable system to know repeat visits of customers, despite having a track of purchase histories.

Online Customer Acquisition

Quite a few technology geeks are employed with online retailing and marketing organizations, who eagerly exercise their capabilities to do online 'snooping' and search engine indexing. They attempt to closely track customers' browsing and search behaviour and successfully direct them to their own websites and offers. The intelligence system of online retailers is mind-blowing. No one can hide from the tracking of information when they are determined to snoop on customers' browsing and purchase behaviour. It is a man-eat-man world out there in the cyber space to grab customers from one another. Search engine indexing is found to help a great deal in the matter of collecting, analysing and storing data for use by the search engine. The search engine index is the location where the collected data is securitized. Technical experts in competing online marketing organizations would work overtime to outsmart each other in designing the most efficient search engine indexing so that their product or service would get precedence and priority over the other in showing up first in the order of search results. Often such competitors pip each other at the post! What may appear first in search results may also stand the chance of gaining the customer view first. Thus, search engine indexing is said to precisely help overcome competition on searches made. The adequacy of the search is dependent on a properly designed search engine index with a plethora mix of key words and linked content, so that information is picked instantly to show on the results page first. Search engine spiders or crawlers, as technologists call them, are said to be deployed to go all around the web universe to enable the search engine index update information in a jiffy.

Online and omnichannel retailing have been the focus of brick-and-mortar retailers in the recent times, while on the other hand, online retailers were trying to open brick-and-mortar stores. Industry experts have opined that this validates the need for the coexistence of one another! Online fashion retailer Myntra recently opened a physical store for its brand 'Roadster' in a partnership with a franchisee in Bengaluru. So, the e-commerce companies seem to place a good deal of trust on brick-and-mortar retailing as well.

Major Models of Online Retail Business in India

The major models of online business carried out successfully in India are of two kinds:

1. The Marketplace Model
2. The Warehouse Model

The Marketplace Model

This model is about an online retailing company which operates by aggregating a number of vendors (by enrolling them as vendors) who have the products/services but transact the sales from the company's web portal but fulfils the delivery of each order from the different vendor points. The best example of this model is Flipkart. Flipkart has innumerable registered vendors. The vendor in this model is also known as 'drop shipper'. So, this model is also known as 'Drop-Shipping Model'. The online sales transactions are managed directly by the company on its web portal. But each vendor makes delivery fulfilments. That means the company receives all the money for the products sold and then after retaining its due margins, Flipkart shares what is due with each vendor.

The Warehouse Model

The warehouse model refers to an online retailing company which operates by storing various products/services and transacts retail sales on the company's web portal including each delivery fulfilment by the company itself. In this model, the online retailer takes the responsibility of selecting the merchandise, managing inventory and fulfilling the delivery of the ordered goods to the customer. This is an investment-intensive model of online retailing. BigBasket is an ideal example of this model of online retailing. The company has established a number of warehouses across India for the purpose of shipping orders on time to customers under its express delivery service. It uses the warehouse model to expand into smaller towns of the country. BigBasket has established warehouses in each metro city where it operates its retail sales network, and one each in many towns as well. Local deliveries of a few fresh items are made effectively through partnerships with neighbourhood stores, where quality of products and timeliness of deliveries are monitored by company personnel.

Future of Online Retailing in India

It is foreseen that consumers may increasingly rely on digital channels to meet their shopping needs. In India, it has been found that there are three factors that drive online retailing and they are smart phone sales, time pressure on consumers and the cost and quality. The Internet has empowered the consumer and is providing information and access across the three stages of purchasing: Information search during the decision-making process, actual purchase transaction and product ownership period including product delivery, maintenance, and return. The evolution of smart phone users and e-commerce makes it possible to buy even food and grocery categories of products online in India. In the past few years, technology breakthroughs have led the retailing industry into new opportunities to exploit online consumers to buy goods and services easily. Easy and secure payment gateways have enabled online shoppers to buy easily. In addition, the newer model of payment such as 'cash on delivery', popularly known as CoD, is a boon to customers as they have the opportunity to see, feel, and check the product before they pay for it.

Retailing in India is going through a new phase of expansion with the adoption of additional models in the online retailing space. Aggressive marketing efforts have been deployed recently by many online retailers such as snapdeal.com, flipkart.com and myntra.com Brick-and-mortar retailers and FMCG companies too have been sprucing up their business, trying to tap into the online segment of customers by using a omnichannel distribution and sales approach to augment their business. It is seen that companies in India are gearing up to reach out to consumers online in a very big way and even traditional FMCG players such as Marico, Dabur, ITC and Bisleri have begun to exploit the huge potential available online.

The Internet has increasingly got integrated into people's everyday life through the smart phones they use. It is a fact that India has been the fastest-growing market with over 530 million smart phone users. The user base is also growing at a whopping 30 per cent plus and the data is available through every telecom and Internet service provider at very negligible and affordable rates. This is sure to propel the success of online retailing in India.

The Success of Flipkart.com

Flipkart is an online retailing company established by its founders Sachin Bansal and Binny Bansal. Although the company was registered in Singapore, it has its headquarters in Bengaluru. From its humble beginnings in 2007, the company has grown by leaps and bounds over the years to clinch the No. 1 position in online retailing in India. Flipkart has adopted the marketplace model. During its tenure of growth, in the last ten plus years, Flipkart has developed a big vendor base who are the backbone of the company's business. Flipkart has been home to many start-up entrepreneurs who sell their products on Flipkart. Companies like Max Fashion, a retail venture of the Landmark Group, Dubai sells its range of products online on Flipkart. The company emerged as a pioneer in online retailing in India. Its disruptive growth is fuelled by its product range width available for the customers and its on-time delivery fulfilment. The focus of Flipkart has been on enlisting a large number of vendors in a wide variety of categories of products. A perfect coordination from the company with the vendors for following up with each order right from the time of its placement till the time of its delivery fulfilment has been the backbone of Flipkart's success in India. Flipkart has adopted a killer pricing strategy, and its prices have been way less than competition, which has won it a large customer base. Competitive pricing is yet a winning strategy adopted by Flipkart along with its positioning of wide product range availability.

Disruptively Innovative CoD System by Flipkart

A few years ago, Flipkart introduced the cash on delivery (CoD) payment system as competition especially from Amazon began to make inroads into the online retail market in India. When all online retailers were offering payment by credit/debit cards only, Flipkart studied the market and boldly introduced the CoD payment system. This means that the customer could pay on receipt of the product. Even though initially the product returns were on the higher side, subsequently this system became popular and many online retailers have adopted it.

Conceptual Promotions at Flipkart

For deep discounting, Flipkart came up with strategic promotional initiatives like the Big Billion Day sales when it offers customers huge deals on mobile phones, cameras, laptops, television sets, home electronics, household appliances, apparel, footwear, etc. apart from additional discounts on the use of specific credit or debit cards. It runs such Big Billion Days for five days during the third week of September every year usually, and this has created a crazy shopping experience for online customers. This deep-discount sale is organized in collaboration with the company's vendors who also share discounts in order to clinch a big quantum of sales. Competing with Flipkart, Amazon has introduced its Great Indian Sale for around four days during the National festival days of India such as the Independence Day and the Republic Day, when discounted special prizes are offered to customers. Amazon also runs such sales campaign during festivals like Diwali known as Great Indian Festival Sale. But at Flipkart, affordable prices are the order of everyday offering price benefits to customers. The Big Billion Day sales set records of sorts every year such as $1 billion sales during the five-day sales period, 1.3 million hand phones sold on a single day and so on. Such is the magnitude of success of the Big Billion Day concept at Flipkart. Flipkart is reported to have registered a 19 per cent growth in revenues in fiscal year ending March 2017 over the previous year with a turnover of over ₹152.64 billion.

A GMV of over ₹60 billion is said to be available onsite in Flipkart for sales. GMV is the sum total value of merchandise available online on the company's portal for sales at any given point in time. GMV has become one of the indicators/parameters of an online company's valuation.and Flipkart is said to be having the highest GMV among Indian online retailing organizations.

In its prime period of business, Flipkart in the recent years acquired Myntra, the fashion online retailing company, which again subsequently acquired Jabong. Flipkart as a group has become a veritable business force to reckon with in the online retail space in India, and it has emerged successfully as undoubtedly the number one online retailer in the country. Innovation coupled with the hard work of putting together a massive product range, enlisting a mammoth vendor base and hosting the largest GMV, all for the benefit of offering value for money to its customers has been catapulting the rapid growth of Flipkart in India!

SECTION II

Ten Success Secrets to Win

Be Determined to Win

SECRET 1

[*Change your thought process of managing a single store to ensuring growth into multiple stores. This will induce the thirst to grow.*]

The first step to win in retailing is to have the determination that you can do it. In India, we see many small- and medium-sized retailers quite widely spread in cities, towns and villages. Most of these are run by their owners or their family members as a single-shop operation for a living. The aim of such a retailer must be to make profits and grow. Sustaining the shop has always been the priority rather than having a thirst to grow every year and make way for more stores. Often small retailers take money out of the business to meet their growing family needs and for small investments for the daughter's wedding or for the son's education. Business growth has never been a priority for small retailers. Funding the growing business has been only from internal accruals, and whenever expenses are made, accruals are hit badly and growth eventually suffers. Hence, these retailers may have been doing the balancing act to sustain the existing store without having a plan to grow. With the growth of the consumer population, especially in the middle-class segment in India, and with banks being ready to offer loans against mortgage, small- and medium-sized retailers can now have adequate financial assistance to make the shop bigger or open new stores in more locations.

Think about Posterity

As the owners view this retail business as insignificant, they often think that the struggle of managing a retail shop should end with their generation and their children should be able to take up office jobs. They have never encouraged their children to enter the retail business, nor have they allowed them to work along with them part-time in the shop whenever time would permit them. So, the business tends to die with the passing of the owner's generation. MSMEs have to introspect and see how their posterity is going to be engaged better in their business. Take the Nadar community retailers of Tamil Nadu. The Nadar shopkeepers, more than half a century ago, took to setting up shops, shunning the 'toddy tapping' their ancestors had done for generations (they thought that their forebears were not in the right business!). They did not bother to grow more palmyrah trees, nor were they inclined to tap toddy any longer. The next generation took to trading in retail and they have been quite successful. The threat for the 'Annachi' retailers of Tamil Nadu is not FDI in retailing but many others including their own posterity. These retailers have slogged it out right from 6 o'clock in the morning till 11 o'clock in the night, serving customers every day. They have known their customers like the back of their palms! Will their children take over their business? The answer is a big No! The children may not like to take over the family business, exactly as their own fathers had refused to take over their ancestors' business of tapping toddy, which gave rise to the faster growth of Indian-made foreign liquor in India! There were no modernized techniques to climb the trees to draw toddy from the palmyrah trees! How many 'Annachis' have grown new palmyrah trees in the last two decades to support tapping toddy? Likewise, the new generation is encouraged to get into newer businesses such as IT and ITES and modern retailing, without trying to take over the family business of small time retailing. One needs to modernize the family retail business in order to make it attractive for the younger generation to jump into.

None of the palmyrah yields were modernized in terms of packaging and distribution for sales. Among the Nadar people, those who were not able or willing to climb trees ventured out to towns from villages, initially to work in small retail shops. They worked their way up, ultimately to become owners of their own businesses. The urge to modernize is simply missing in their earlier business as well as the current business of shop keeping.

Organize the Business to Attract the Next Generation

WITCO was a small-time shop in George Town, Chennai, selling plasticware, travel bags and accessories. It was opened first in 1951 by the late Mr M. P. C. Mohamed. His son Mr V. P. Harris took over the business and focused on retailing by opening more WITCO stores. The company has 15 stores currently. WITCO has now become a brand in the travel accessories and luggage segment, and the third generation has now taken over to manage the business growth. Even some grocery and *kirana* retailers have made their shops bigger and attractive for their children to take over and run the stores.

Believe in a Great Business Opportunity

Consumption is growing in India. People consume a lot. Unlike the bygone years when people's consumption was limited because of paucity and unaffordability, today the quantum and the variety of consumption have increased a lot. Recently, a television show hosted a debate between two groups of people. The subject of the debate was whether men or women as consumers nowadays buy more than what they actually need. The conclusion of the debate came as a no-brainer that everyone in their own ways buys more than they need. During the debate, many instances emerged where people bought products they never used or bought products in more quantities than what they actually needed. Even when consumers buy food products, they often buy the routine stuff and along with that they also buy the new stuff to try out. Ladies often buy sarees and salwars in good numbers nowadays. A mere change of attitude urging people to wear varieties as fashion changes or as movies would introduce new trends, may impact the enormity and frequency of purchases! After all, as we do not have a mind in India to throw away old stuff soon, our wardrobes always keep swelling and enlarging! An aunt of mine keeps balancing the number of sarees she has in stock as she gives away an old one for charity for every new one she buys—an exceptional case though!

Consumption Induced by Manufacturers

There has always been a meticulous plan devised to increase consumption in India. Manufacturers have been good at it. Toothpaste used to be consumed in a miserly manner in the past as the aluminium nozzle of the tubes was so narrow that it would push out paste in less quantity. A little wider now, the nozzles release more paste on the same length of toothbrush bristles, increasing consumption. The introduction of shampoos in sachets in India introduced the concept of shampooing the hair even in our remotest villages. Broken into smaller pieces for easier consumption, the effort of innovatively selling every other product in a sachet has increased consumption in every corner of our vast country. When we talk of consumption, our customers need not face the situation of dearth that they faced a couple of decades ago. As products and services are available in abundance and as quite often the media tells us how to use them, we buy things in abundance. The once-used small refrigerators in homes are no longer seen in households, and we see only pretty large ones now that can facilitate more storage, proving the point that the more we buy the more we store and consume.

> We are good at what we are and let us strengthen our domestic retailing skills to win over customers.

Consumption Triggered by Modern Retailers

Retailers are doing their part to increase consumption. Increased displays, free-access shelving that instantaneously provides an access to every product in store, bundled offers, cross promotions, up-selling (converting a burger order into a value meal), etc. are a few vivid efforts taken to increase consumption on the retail floors. A few retailers regularly announce schemes to turn in the old for new in order to help customers make space for additional items in their wardrobes! Retailers also go ahead with their multichannel efforts to reach out to customers while they try and expand quickly into smaller towns. As the mid-segment grows in an incredible measure in India, we can expect future budgets of the Government of India to keep raising the taxable income slab.

Bank on Your Own Strengths

Recently, a friend and I took a walk in the busy Ranganathan street of Chennai to have a glimpse of what is happening in the

Mecca of retailing, as they call it! As we walked into Saravana Stores, a floor manager greeted us offering us help to take us around, guessing rightly that we had come to take a look! The merchandise categories are so relevant to the target customers that Saravana Stores have got the model right! A Walmart may find it next to impossible to make a tie-up with the seven hundred 'artisans' and *karigars* that Saravana works with for over two decades now! The compelling sales strategies for the 100 varieties of sarees ranging from 'Kushboo Cotton' to 'Kerala Zaris' at the best prices can never be organized by any retailer who comes through the FDI route! The Saravana Stores began as a very small retail store as we all know, but today by dint of the sheer focus on retailing to specific segments of native customers understanding clearly their needs, the store is a great force to reckon with, and will be so for any modern or multinational retailer.

Case 1: Easyday is a chain of supermarkets now run by the Future Group. The Easyday stores were launched in Punjab for the last few years and they did not crack the model to be rolled out successfully across the country until Bharti Retail forged a merger with Future Retail to deploy their combined strengths to grow into many cities, yet they have not achieved any significant national presence across India.

Case 2: When Bata started retailing in India, the company achieved a nation-wide spread with their small stores (which ultimately numbered almost 1,200 across the country) and small traditional footwear stores sprang up around them in many markets, expanding the market size itself! The small footwear stores in the local markets coexisted and thrived because Bata's wholesale division also efficiently supplied them with their products through their well-networked distributors.

Having said that, it may be very difficult to manage small stores in large numbers for foreign retailers in India, as they have to understand local merchandise preferences thoroughly, which is a difficult task. Added to that will come the woes of servicing a large and wide supply chain. India is such a vast country, where, leave alone foreign retailers, even Indian large retailers have found it next to impossible to get the assortment right. That would be the biggest edge for the local traditional retailers.

Mr T. Thanushgaran, chairman of Shri Kannan Departmental Store, who has organized to retail more than 15 varieties of 'idli podis', 'vadahams' and 'pappadams' in each of his stores, is a unique phenomenon by himself on the retailing landscape of South India. He subtly sells a few varieties of dry fish in a remote corner in the store, redefining and rediscovering the right adjacencies for the vegetarian categories to steer clear of the non-vegetarian ones! Any multinational store may find it difficult to organize its categories specific to every store's customer preferences. Let the 'Annachi retailers' of Tamil Nadu rework their strategies to become successful amidst competition from multinationals. Let them welcome FDI in retailing but forge closer associations with their customers. Let them modernize their stores in such a way that the youngsters in their families are encouraged to take to retailing! It may be a matter of 'sail or sink' for many retailers as multinationals may start spreading across the country soon. Collaborative buying by small retailers by teaming together can work wonders! And many other strategies can be adopted by small- and medium-sized retailers so that they can grow par excellence as compared to their foreign or large retail counterparts or competitors!

They should just be determined to grow!

Blending Intelligence with Determination: Khadim's, Kolkata

After attempting to start a business of his own, the hardworking Shri Satya Prasad Roy Burman, the late founder and chairman of Khadim India bought a small footwear shop in Chitpur, Kolkata in 1965, then operating by the name, K. M. Khadim. This small step taken by him ultimately resulted in the creation of the invincible footwear retail chain, Khadim's.

At a time when branded products were scarce, he put his vision first, to build a big footwear retail business. Shri Burman identified the right people and worked with them at the most basic levels of footwear manufacturing. In this effort, he developed a team of footwear artisans. He believed that the success of his business rested upon building a good manufacturing and sourcing base. If he had to fulfil his vision of selling footwear to the masses, he had to develop a robust back-end supply base. His strength was his ability to work with humble manufacturers, giving them support and encouraging them to make good quality footwear. He played a major role in transforming the local footwear manufacturers who were given a significantly good livelihood by his manufacturing orders and his personal guidance. All his cocreated entrepreneurs and the business community began to fondly refer to him as 'Barobabu'. Known for his stature as the father figure of many small footwear manufacturers, he had a keen desire to coach them so that they grew together. His passion to nurture small manufacturers became evident when he once said, 'More than being a manufacturer, I love to manufacture manufacturers'. Such was his determination to work with manufacturers. His success is attributed to his belief in blending 'intelligence with determination'.

Shri Burman walked across shops in the market to sell his footwear. Because he ensured good quality in all that he made through his team of small manufacturers, there was a good demand for his products. His imagination could render many different styles, which differentiated his merchandise from competition. What is currently known as B2B was his business forte. He created two strong networks _ on the one hand, he built his wholesale network fast and, on the other, he was strengthening his network of small footwear manufacturing entrepreneurs spreading steadily in Kolkata and in the rest of West Bengal. He spotted an opportunity in the less-crowded branded footwear segment and began to supply footwear to various retail outlets going into many towns of the Eastern region. He soon organized his business well and made it into a corporate entity in 1981. He was very keen to understand customer needs and plan his range of footwear sourcing accordingly. As the founder, he played a key role in shaping the destiny of Khadim's into an organized retail business par excellence.

Shri Burman travelled the length and breadth of the locations of his outsourced manufacturing network and his marketplace that had both rapidly spread over larger territories. He had an obsession for understanding consumer psychology, which made him hit the bull's eye in his planning to provide the right products at the right time, in the right price, in the right mix and at the right time. Giving good quality products at affordable prices was the principal mission that he set forth for achieving his business objectives.

Determined as he was, Shri Burman garnered the gall to compete in a growing but competitive market for branded footwear. The early 1990s saw the economic liberation and with it came the retail revolution as well. Many organized entities began to open exclusive brand retail outlets. Footwear was one of the major categories that rode the success of exploiting organized retailing opportunities. Bata was fast expanding its modern retailing network as many others too did in India. Shri Burman set his eyes on retailing to come closer to consumers. He knew well that it was only by creating a retail network, he could deliver products to customers and understand their feedback first-hand from them. He opened the first Khadim's retail store in 1993 in Kolkata. Since then he expanded the retail chain in two major models _ company owned and company operated and franchise owned and company operated. Shri Burman laid a robust foundation for Khadim's business whose strengths reposed in a wide market presence through a well-built dealer-distributor network and company-owned retail stores combined with the flexibility of an established trader-cum-manufacturing model. This is the secret of the success of Khadim's brand equity built over the years.

With the support of his son, Mr Siddhartha Roy Burman, Shri Burman made his stride into the various states of the country making Khadim's a popular footwear brand among many retailers and customers alike. With his insightful attention to technology as well as consumer psychology, Shri Burman prepared the organization to face challenges of any kind. It is his indomitable and unstinted drive that has helped Khadim's become one of the market leaders in organized footwear manufacturing and retailing in India. A huge asset that the brand is, Shri Satya Prasad Roy Burman left a legacy in the Khadim's brand, big enough for his son Mr Siddhartha Roy Burman to continue the journey of his business success, as he expired in 2013.

The brand made inroads in South India faster than expected. Khadim's now has the largest presence in East India, and it is considered as one of the top three footwear players in South India. The brand also boasts of the largest footwear retail franchise network in India (Technopak Report 2016). As of 2017, Khadim's operates close to 853 branded exclusive retail stores (bulk of which are franchised), across 23 states and 1 union territory in India, Puducherry, and has a network of 370 distributors who cater to the multitude of retailers across India.

Mr Siddhartha Roy Burman, saddled as the chairman and managing director of Khadim's, has been doing no less a job than his father in taking Khadim's through its well-chartered growth trajectory. With his fascination for retailing and his drive to identify himself with the customers, he makes it a point to visit the shop floors to interact subtly with many customers to understand their needs and preferences. Retaining its original strategies of success, Mr Siddhartha Roy Burman is now chalking out his all-India strategy of attaining more retail touch points to retail products at affordable price points!

Key Takeaways from Khadim's

- Building a robust manufacturing and sourcing back-end is a key success factor of the retail business.

- Small and simple manufacturers can be of great help if one coaches them on making good quality products.

- A sustained team effort with the determination to cocreate products can give a differentiated edge to win over competition.

- An entrepreneur must not stop with his initial success, but be determined to take the business to the next level, as Shri Burman went on to open his own retail store without resting on the success he achieved in his B2B business.

- Be determined to build a robust business by working on its operational details that can stand the test of time.

- Imagination if combined with determination can produce great results.

Choose the Right Location

SECRET 2

[*The famous adage on retail location goes thus: 'The three most important factors that contribute to the success of a retail store are location, location and location'.*]

To win in retailing, it is of utmost significance to choose the right location. In fact, retail experts say that the three most important factors that contribute to the success of a retail store are location, location and location. That's the way someone put it emphatically to underscore the importance of location in retailing. Often when one tries to open a retail store, one may think of one's own conveniences and accessibility. But the foremost consideration for new retailers must be to put themselves in the customers' shoes and think what location would be convenient for them to access the store. A good location can *make a store* and a bad location can *break a store*.

Going by the 'Gut Feel'

Small- and medium-sized retailers while looking for shop premises usually go with their 'gut feel' to identify location for the proposed store. The store should be established in a location where footfalls happen for sure because of the already existing shopping environment there. The 'gut feel' approach is seen as a common phenomenon as people scout for retail properties to lease for establishing the store. This approach is squarely based on the experience of the retailer in the area to understand the market, and the success would be based on the correctness of the understanding.

Going by References

Friends who are retailers also usually suggest the right location based on their experiences and 'gut feel'. Friends who are in the location may guide new retailers who look for the right location. People with no experience in running a retail store may seek guidance of the local friends who already have researched many locations and retail properties and analysed their prospects for doing successful business there. Such referential location guidance may run a risk as the selection is based on someone else's experience and ideas. The local property agents give references as well. They would have already researched the potential of locations and come up with the appropriate properties. The risk again reposes on the availability of a range of properties with the agent and the property agent may hard sell an unworthy location.

Creating a Checklist

One of the most appropriate methods of choosing the right location for a new store is by analysing the factors that may contribute to a successful location and listing them down. Based on the list, the prospective retailer may come up with a few questions creating a checklist from a customer point of view.

- *Is the proposed area convenient for customers to shop?* A location is said to be convenient only when there are no barriers for customers to walk into that location. Customers are now aware of markets and products. They are mobile as each household in any kind of town, small town or village in India has a two-wheeler. If the location is conducive for shopping many things in one place like a marketplace, then the location may be convenient for customers. A research report on locational convenience says, 'Factors such as time scarcity, the changing role of women and the increasing number of male shoppers have also combined to create a generation of consumers that will no longer tolerate inconvenient shopping locations'.

- *Is the area well lit during nights?* Lighting in a location during nights and safety are interlinked needs. If the entire location is well lit and bright, customers would view the location as safe for shopping during late evenings and nights. The retailer could check whether the entire area is bright and safe.
- *Is the area safe for customers to walk around and shop?* The retailer must understand whether the area is known for any untoward incidents. Even if it is a popular location but if it is known as an area where untoward incidents have happened, it would make sense to avoid such a location. Safety is one criteria customers would never be willing to compromise while shopping, as many customers for small and medium retailers could be women.
- *How good are the footfalls in the area?* One can stand in the area and count customers walking into the shopping area every hour during the week and weekends. This is the simplest way of understanding footfalls. The other method is to count footfalls in similar stores in the location during peak and lean hours and during weekdays and weekends. High footfall areas have been proved to be successful locations for retailing in India. The efforts of the retailer could focus only on bringing the visitors to the area to just enter the store. Advertising expenses also could be minimal because of the already available footfalls and one does not have to advertise or promote the store heavily to bring customers to the area.
- *Are there enough houses/apartments in the nearby radius of the location?* It is advisable to take stock of the number of houses

and apartments in the vicinity, say of a few kilometres radius of the store. The more the number of households the more could be the footfalls into the store. Customers in the nearby catchment areas could play a huge role in the success of a retail store as they could be the captive ones with stickiness for the store. A friendly neighbourhood store is always successful. Catchment stores in colonies get the opportunity to know customers quite closely and forge a healthy relationship for long.

- *How many customers would visit a similar store in the area every day?* Just like one would count footfalls in a marketplace, one can count the footfalls that happen in similar kinds of stores in the same area. As part of the research efforts taken for identifying the location for the store, the study of footfalls in similar and competing stores must be done by counting them during peak and lean hours and during weekdays and weekends.
- *What is the average sale per day of similar stores in the area?* Similarly, buying conversion from footfalls can be calculated by counting the number of people who carry items or bagful of items bought from the store. By an enquiry into the average bill value, by sheer intelligence one can also find out how much could be the average value of purchases made by each customer, which in other words is ticket size. If there are 100 customer footfalls, 80 out of them buy at an average value of ₹200, then the store sales per day can be calculated as 80 × 200 = ₹16,000. The new retailer may plan his daily sales by using this technique for forecasting his sales in the location. This calculation in a few locations may render a comparative analysis of store and its location performance.
- *Is the shop location situated within a busy marketplace?* A busy marketplace would bring in ready footfalls as mentioned earlier. The cost of real estate is high in busy marketplaces but the higher rates of sales would help stores in busy marketplaces

perform well. A trade-off needs to be weighed between the cost of location and the revenues the store can churn out. For small- and medium-sized retail stores, it would make sense to locate themselves in busy marketplaces unlike destination stores which could be located in far-flung areas.

- *Is the location in an odour-free area?* While choosing a location, care should be taken to check for the location to be free from dirt and bad odour. However small the stores would be the customers would buy from them only if they are located in a clean and neat environment. Sometimes busy marketplaces may carry out various activities that may pose challenges for maintaining the area clean. If such areas disseminate bad odour, one should avoid opening the store there.
- *Can customers see my store?* 'Joh dikhta hai, woh bikta hai' is the famous mantra for successful retailing. That means 'what is visible, sells'! First, the store should be visible for customers even from a reasonable distance. So, the location ought to be such that the entire store right from its signage through the façade must be visible to customers. This means the store location should be 'eye-catching'. The point is that the customer should not have to search for the store. It is mandatory for the retailer to establish his store in a clearly visible location.
- *Is there enough frontage for the store so that customers can see the signboard easily?* It is the frontage of the store where the store signage is put up. This must be adequately large to place the signboard. The permanent advertising board for the store is its signage. The bigger the signage area available in the store premises, the better is its performance. So, the location and store property should be checked for visibility and frontage clarity.
- *Is there enough space for customers to park their two-wheelers near the shop?* In today's time, almost all customers have

their own two-wheelers and cars. Customers seek the convenience of parking when they visit stores. Even in small retail outlets, they expect a few two-wheeler parking spaces. Retailers must look for locations where there is parking for two-wheelers available just around the store premises. Customers do not like to walk a long distance to visit any store.

- *Can customers walk into my store easily?* It is only fair for a prospective retailer to check if the area around the store is free from barriers for pedestrians. People do not like to brave any blocks or barriers. If the store location is just by the side of a one-way road, customers may like to shop only along the direction of the traffic flow. They would not park their cars on one side of the road and then cross over to access the store if the store is located in the opposite direction of the one-way road. Care must be taken to see that the location/area chosen allows free movement of customers towards the store entrance. If the height of the building is more it may make sense to avoid such locations. Customers may not be willing to climb a number of steps to enter the store. Similarly, they may not like to go underground to shop as they may consider it inconvenient to enter. Customers may not voice many of these inconveniences but research has established that they deter customers from entering the store.
- *Is there enough pillar-free space within the store for ensuring customer convenience?* This question pertains to the store property. If the small store has many pillars inside, it may affect the visibility of the whole interior of the store. The visibility of shelves and displays would also be affected, and customers may not be able to see the merchandise nor the various transparent activities like weighing inside the store. So, it is necessary for the store to have clear space inside.

Riding Piggyback on an Already Successful Location

Choosing a location that can ride biggyback on an already established and successful destination also would help. For instance, if the store is located near a movie theatre or near the bus or railway station where there are already assured footfalls, the store may be successful. This parasitic location choice would depend on the nature of the store. Shops usually ride piggyback on successful restaurants, educational institutions, theatres, choultries, shop clusters in colonies, office complexes, etc.

Location Analysis

Location search includes economic and business considerations for every location in consideration. It finally amounts to the feasibility of a particular location for a particular store so that the sales revenues forecast for the location would yield enough margins for the store to grow. Location analysis involves three steps beginning with customer analysis, locating the trade area and finally the right property selection in the trade area. Research studies suggest that the factors determining the business potential at a particular location can largely be attributed to those such as the possibility for economies of scale, the demographic and lifestyle characteristics, the spending capacity, the competition and finally one's own capability to handle store operations at a particular location. The final location is a sum total of these aforementioned factors.

The economy of scale comes into picture when a retailer is capable of acquiring multiple locations and, subsequently, takes advantage of the situation. For example, a retailer having two stores in the same suburb at separate locations can use a single billboard for advertising and promotions. This is an example of how a retailer can make use of economies of scale to reduce operational costs. Such scale can also result in increased buying capability for the stores and the retailer may purchase at bargain prices consequent to such scale. The demographic and lifestyle characteristics at a particular location should be given equal importance, as they may determine the spending patterns of the target customers. Some of the retailers may consider factors like festivals in a particular region so that an estimate of the high selling periods and the consequent increase in sales figures can also be determined. The researching retailers may arrive at a location quotient (LQ), an index created with the factors mentioned earlier and use the same to compare the capabilities of various locations. LQ also may give an idea on whether a certain group of people with particular characteristics inhabits a particular location in a certain area. This may help retailers in understanding the profile of the probable customers and compare the same with the positioning of the product or service that the retailer plans to offer. To sum up the key takeaways, an attractive location is expected to be easily accessible; free of any customer and product movement barriers; having good visibility and having good traffic flow besides having parking facilities. Deciding on a well-researched location would give the retailer an immediate advantage over competition, while it could decrease the risk involved and increase acceptance from prospective customers while entering a new market.

Think Futuristic

While choosing the location for a prospective retail store, one ought to have in mind not only the present but also the future. The location must be current and good, fulfilling all the basic requirements that make a good location. A futuristic location would take into consideration the growing customer catchments in the location and nearby too. Today's good location may not be tomorrow's good location. The pace of growth of towns and even villages has been very high. The establishment of roads and the related new housing developments along with the extension of connectivity networks has created new areas of colonization. This expansion has created new markets for retailers. The growth of towns has paved the way for the establishment of larger bazaars and new high streets. So, the retailer should always be ready to relocate their stores as customers and markets may move to newer locations.

Starting Small: Hatti Food and Beverages Pvt. Ltd (Hatti Kaapi), Bengaluru

Mahendar hails from a family of coffee growers who were planters for generations in and around the district of Hassan, Karnataka. In the 1950s, post-independence, his great grandfather lost the business for some reason. So, his father had to quit coffee growing and with the remaining fortune he started the then popular transport business. As a private bus operator, he was doing very well along with his brothers, until one fine day the business was taken over by the State Transport Corporation all of a sudden. Along with the takeover came the job offer for his father from the State Transport Corporation. He had no other option than to accept it for the sake of the family and this, according to Mahendar, actually killed his father's love for doing business. 'I was a mute spectator to the woes of my working father who had to work and do everything to make our family happy. But, the business instinct remained in me and as a young boy I was adventurous. I never wanted to work for anyone and my eyes were set on doing a business', avers Mahendar. He says that he often used to express to his father, the thought of doing business again, and his father, although encouraged him, emphasized that Mahendar should be educated first and then go about doing any business. Though Mahendar did well in both studies and sports, his focus was on doing some business or the other. He represented the under-16 cricket team of Karnataka. Smartness was just second skin to him. After his pre-university, he joined graduation studies in electronics and before he finished the course, he dropped out. He confessed to his father that he was forcing himself to study, when his sincere intent was to do business. Understanding him completely, Mahendar's father relented to his wish but told him sternly that he should always adopt the following two principles in his business life:

- Do your business by ethical means always.
- Behavioural integrity should be the identity quotient for yourself.

Even to this day, Mahendar says that he keeps following these principles to the letter, come what may. He was just 19, brimming with self-confidence and raring to go to the competitive world of business. While weighing several options, he came across his friend's father who was into the trading of coffee beans. He sought his advice and began small time trading in coffee beans, as that was the only commodity he could lay his hands on immediately. He took trading to the next level with ease by sourcing coffee beans locally and supplying them to exporters, which did not require much capital investment. One of the suppliers even supported him in the trade by financing him to source on a larger scale. His business grew, but it took the form of hedging, over time. He earned a lot of money but did not have peace of mind, as he thought that this trading required a great deal of speculation, which again added to his stress, and was against the ethics he had imbibed. Trading, he felt was just like gambling, and to the surprise of many of his friends, he quit the business abruptly even when he was doing well.

He had his fingers crossed; his aim was to develop a business and not just earn money. He came across another friend at this juncture, Srikant, who informed him about a co-packing opportunity with Tata Coffee in Bengaluru that could be taken up if he was interested. Mahendar saw the allied nature of this new assignment to the coffee business that he has been used to. He also dreamt of dealing in roasted coffee beans and supplying them to restaurants in many places. When this opportunity came his way, he replied in the affirmative to Srikant who introduced him to the relevant people in Tata Coffee, Bengaluru. Mahendar was all set to get into the new business and establish a blending unit. He had by then lost his father and being the only child to his parents, he was keen on taking his mother wherever he went. He moved to Bengaluru in 1993 with his mother and his close friend M. L. Gowda who was also his neighbour. Both of them even today remain inseparable through thick and thin. Gowda was part of Mahendar's family and the three of them relocated to the city of Bengaluru. Mahendar's mother gave her complete support and she and her sisters (Mahendar's aunts) even gave their jewels to be pledged to raise money for the new business. Srikant left Bengaluru for Mysore after he made the required introductions in Tata Coffee to Mahendar. Mahendar was waiting for the orders of production from Tata Coffee after he established his small blending facility but the authorities did not release any order and, consequently, he did not know what to do. When Mahendar tried to push his way to get the orders, the Tata Coffee unit manager Bopanna turned his back on Mahendar and said that they would call him only when there was a need.

Mahendar felt disappointed as he had already availed loans to buy blending equipment based on earlier promises. Whenever the thought of going back to the coffee bean trading business came to his mind, he chased it away firmly. He had learnt the art of exercising perseverance from his grandfather who had said, 'Never stop making an attempt'. Appropriately, Mahendar thought that he would once again knock at the doors of Tata Coffee. He did. His security friend at the gate welcomed him and that was the first positive sign there for him. Bopanna met him with warmth and Mahendar told him that he came with dreams and if an opportunity was given to him he would prove his mettle. Though he did not have the coffee co-packing opportunity then to be given to Mahendar, he said that he was shortlisting vendors for sourcing badam (almond) pre-mix and that if he could come with samples the next day for trials, there would be a chance for Mahendar to make it to the list of sourcing partners for Tata Coffee. Mahendar and Gowda had no clue about how to make badam mix, but they worked hard to make it after returning to their unit with a general understanding that it was a mix of pulverized sugar with milk and badam powder in the right proportion. They checked out the big brands available in the market along with the locally made ones. Mahendar was a quality freak! They sourced good quality badam, good quality refined sugar and premium quality milk powder. They made blend after blend throughout the night and came up with a mix to be presented for trials scheduled at 4 pm that day. After spending a sleepless night, Mahendar was ready with his sample and presented himself to Bopanna by 3 pm itself, an hour earlier than the appointed time. The samples from all prospective suppliers were put on trials with 35 people tasting for giving their feedback, post a blind test. It was a 45-minute tasting and testing session and those 45 minutes, according to Mahendar, were like 45 days! Bopanna declared the results and he told Mahendar with a pat on his back that his product was the best and that he was in, as a supplier. He suggested a few improvements. Tata Coffee placed their first order of 35 kg of badam pre-mix and that day was a day of celebration for both Mahendar and Gowda; they had a feast with the ₹35 that they were left with, after they had spent on the new product development! The first lot was supplied to the market through the various depots and the feedback was good. Mahendar laid emphasis on consistency in the delivery of quality. The product was well accepted and the order went up to 100 kg a month.

Soon other pre-mixes were added to the order_instant coffee, tea pre-mix, soups, etc. Mahendar was very clear that he would make each product following the exact quality formulations without cutting corners anywhere and that made the trick to click with Tata Coffee. The orders from Tata Coffee soon soared from 5_6 tonnes a month to 60_70 tonnes, sometimes touching even 100 tons. Mahendar became the number one supplier to Tata Coffee. Mahendar was impressed with the code of conduct and ethics of Tata Coffee and according to him, it was only quality that always mattered with the company and nothing else. Even today his business has been a roaring success for Mahendar and currently he is the only outsourced supplier for pre-mixes in the whole country for Tata Coffee. Mahendar says that many people emphasize on quality as a watchword, but true success lies only in one's ability to put quality delivery in practice always.

Notwithstanding this success, Mahendar wanted to stabilize himself and his business further. His dreams were about selling coffee as a beverage. As Mahendar and Gowda walked the streets of Bengaluru, they discussed coffee often. On the one hand, they were amazed at how restaurants such as Café Darshini and MTR offered good quality South Indian filter coffee but coffee was only a small part of their entire food business. Mahendar thought that he could offer better filter coffee in an exclusive retail service format at less prices for the consumer using his knowledge and experience of coffee blends. On the other hand, he was also witnessing the growth of Café Coffee Day in Bengaluru more as a place to hang out! He wanted to offer only good coffee, no conversations! Both Gowda and Mahendar now got into the act of making blends and putting them to trials with their friends. They made blends after blends and took feedbacks after trials, because obtaining feedbacks has always helped him make better quality products than his competitors! Mahendar says, 'The Spark that I had in me was this: I'll bring tasty filter coffee to my customers exclusively with a focus on serving them at an affordable price'.

Mahendar's trials were successful and now he needed the right people to be associated with him. He says that God has been kind to him in showing the right people at the right time. He came across one Mr Lakshmana Swamy who retired from MTR as a marketing head and who had earlier worked for Unilever as well. After meeting him, Mahendar wanted him to join him. Lakshmana Swamy had declined many such offers earlier but according to Mahendar he instantly agreed to work with him on this project. Mahendar took his blend to Adigas, a popular chain of South Indian restaurants in Bengaluru, as he saw an opportunity to supply coffee blend to all his restaurants. Adigas came forward to let him do the trials first with beverages made out of his blends, before buying them. So, they asked Mahendar and M. L. Gowda to serve filter coffee beverages as trials to Adigas' customers in the morning hours every day. Mahendar and Lakshmana Swamy would wake up early morning and serve coffee to customers in Adigas starting as early as 5 am to get their feedback while M. L. Gowda used to take care of the back-end operations. They shared the good feedback with the promoters and expected an order from them but the order did not come. A striking quality of Mahendar is his ability to follow up with perseverance, and he went to the Adigas promoters a few weeks later. To his dismay, they said that they did not place the order as their quality was 'not good'. Mahendar felt very bad as his trials were met with very good feedback. The truth was that a relative of the promoters was supplying coffee powder. This motivated Mahendar to look at better avenues to market his coffee powder. They thought of opening their own coffee outlets as they knew that the true quality verdict was given by the end consumer always and they thought why not go to them!

A hunt for a small space to serve coffee began and they hit upon a 30 square feet space in the busy Gandhi Bazaar Street owned by a man rendering documentation service with a typewriting machine. Mahendar believes in sharing quite a lot, and the moment Mahendar offered ₹1 per cup of coffee that he sold, the man agreed to give away his space on lease. Having got a small place, Mahendar and Lakshmana Swamy put their heads together to form a new brand as they knew how a brand name could work for building their business. They met a friend, Rajesh Achar, who had a graphic design business, Art Focus. At the request of Mahendar and based on his brief of the South Indian Filter Coffee offering, Rajesh came up the next day with a list of 14 brand name options and logos/mascots and he had highlighted one and that was Hatti Kaapi. Hatti means a group of houses, a home in a village, and Kaapi means coffee. The mascot Rajesh had done for this brand name was an old traditional Brahmin sitting and blending the meter coffee beverage. All the brand elements were, thus, decided and the signboard soon came up on the premises in the Gandhi Bazaar Street. On 27 November 2009, Mahendar served the first coffee to an old man who visited the shop first. As the area was a very native South Indian dominated one, people had a flair and taste for good filter coffee and they would not take any coffee just like that. The man sipped the coffee, paid the money and went his way. When Mahendar asked for his feedback, he just mentioned 'good' before he went from the shop. At around 7.30 am, the man who had the very first cup of coffee came back asking for one more cup! Mahendar says that the very return of the same customer a second time was the true feedback he got about the quality of his product. Sales went up drastically from the 300 cups they sold the first day to 3,000 cups a day and the other nearby established South Indian restaurants serving coffee had to shudder at the competition that Hatti Kaapi was posing to them. Mahendar offered coffee at ₹5 and even upma at ₹5, which meant that breakfast came at ₹10 in total. This attracted a lot of customers. His landlord became very happy as he was making ₹3,000 every day which amounted to more than ₹90,000 a month! Mahendar now hired a person by the name Uday from Café Darshini after meeting up with the café owner seeking his permission to hire the boy; Mahendar had to settle the small advances that Uday had got from his previous owner. The team was set and Hatti Kaapi was rocking. But soon trouble started. While Hatti Kaapi served good quality filter coffee at ₹5 a cup, restaurants sold coffee of mediocre quality at ₹7 a cup. Pressure from competitive quarters mounted for Mahendar with politicians getting involved in the fray to get him go out of the premises soon. Notices were served to him almost every day for the wrong reasons of creating a 'crowd' in the neighbourhood and soon Mahendar had to vacate the premises under pressure. This set him to think that he should open many outlets in Bengaluru.

Every setback gave him a shot in his arm to expand and grow. The first proof of the concept was successful; although Mahendar had the option to fight every notice, he did not want to spend precious time in any litigations. So, he shut shop in the first location with tears in his eyes. Mahendar now thanks all those who created trouble as those hurdles rekindled his vision to grow in other available high streets. He opened three more such small outlets with the help of the funding of ₹500,000 made by the Corporation Bank. Mahendar recalls that he received a call from one Mr Vikrant, facilities Manager at Infosys Headquarters. Having tasted Hatti Kaapi's filter coffee, he invited Mahendar for a session of 'trials' and 'feedback', and it was a thrilling experience for him to do that. His filter coffee competed during the trials with those of Kamath's and the likes. He got the good news that Hatti Kaapi gained space in the premises to open a counter. In a place where there were 23,000 employees, it was a great opportunity for Hatti Kaapi to open a shop to sell coffee at ₹5 a cup! Hatti Kaapi became a big success in Infosys, and within the next 5 years the brand opened 17 shops in almost all the branch office premises of Infosys_Hyderabad, Bengaluru, Mysore, etc. Mahendar recalls with gratitude the opportunity offered by Infosys, which served the twin purposes of serving good coffee for its employees at an affordable price and at the same time helping Hatti Kaapi grow.

Success begets success. The quality consciousness at Hatti Kaapi and its sustained service standards paved the way to open an outlet at the Bengaluru International Airport. The store was quite a popular one, which was very busy almost round the clock! A member of the parliament was so amazed to experience the taste of good filter coffee at ₹15 a cup in the Bengaluru airport that he queried in a session why the government should not take steps to serve good coffee at the country's other airports too, through such quality outlets at affordable prices as Hatti Kaapi. Mahendar says that good quality always gets noticed and attracts appreciation with customers. His people line up is awesome now _ everyone has joined Hatti Kaapi, motivated solely by the passion to work for the brand. Besides M. L. Gowda, Rajesh the graphic designer and Lakshmana Swamy (who is 84 years old now, visiting minimum 2 outlets of Hatti Kaapi every day!). Mahendar has M. S. Narayan, ex-CFO of GMR Projects as the director finance, Venkata Girish (IIM, Kolkata), former Jet Airways employee and a die-hard fan of Hatti Kaapi as director sales and operations, Sadashiva from rural Karnataka and Shivaram Malavalli as mentors and Sampath who takes care of the senior citizens' club and the differently abled initiative at Hatti Kaapi, in his able management team.

Mahendar's wife Smitha Mahendar and Gowda's wife Manjula Gowda, both homemakers, supported their husbands in their venture thoroughly at every step, along with their children Namish Mahendar, Ruhika Mahendar and Harshini Gowda, Amith Gowda. According to Mahendar, great family support could alleviate any business tension! Mahendar says that he is delighted to see his mother, Mrs Rajani Sudhakar lighting the lamp on the inauguration of every Hatti Kaapi outlet. Around 25 per cent of Hatti Kaapi's employees are senior citizens and differently abled people. Mahendar is very particular about giving back to society in whatever manner possible. With close to 250 employees currently and marching towards a century in number soon from the current 45 outlets, Hatti Kaapi's vision as expressed by Mahendar is to go global now and he says with a grin, 'I want Hatti Kaapi to be served in America, brewed by Americans!'

Key Takeaways from Hatti Kaapi

- Move out of your comfort zone and relocate if necessary to avail better business opportunities.
- Never give up on initial failures. Perseverance in following your passion pays for sure.
- Do your business ethically with a view to truly help people involved in every facet of it.
- Quality should not only become the watchword for your business, but you ought to apply quality in practice sincerely.
- Customers are your bouncing boards. Get their feedback tirelessly and improve quality of your products and services.
- When any door closes, another door of greater opportunity definitely opens. Grab that opportunity and progress beyond failures.
- Always begin small to see bigger results in the retail business.
- People are key to the retail business. Work with them and reward them.
- Stay with family values. They would pay in business.

Know Your Customers

SECRET 3

> *A customer is the most important visitor on our premises.*
> *He is not dependent on us. We are dependent on him.*
> *He is not an interruption to our work. He is the purpose of it.*
> *He is not an outsider in our business. He is part of it.*
> *We are not doing him a favour by serving him. He is doing us a favour by giving us an opportunity to do so.*
> —Mahatma Gandhi

The Indian retailer practises the true meaning of relationship. Many years ago, I remember, I had forgotten to buy some products for my home—a list of sundry items my wife had paged me to buy. I was returning from office that day, when suddenly I remembered the forgotten shopping assignment. But before I could realize, I had almost reached my residential complex and it was pretty late too for me at the end of the day to hunt for a supermarket nearby. I looked intently at my pager and read the message again and as I was doing it, I instantly realized that there was a small neighbourhood retail store by the name Cheap & Best within the Raheja Vihar premises where we were residing in suburban Mumbai.

Accessing the store was easy, though I had to walk a few steps down the pedestrian walkway to reach the store counters. A few customers were in the shop. The shopkeeper was busy attending to them. In the midst of his business of attending to a customer, I could see him smile at me in a warm gesture of welcoming me there. I too smiled at him as I went through the list I had in my pager. I carefully ordered all the items. My enthusiasm to buy ran riot once I saw the array of items in the shelves. No sooner had I picked up a number of them to my heart's content then I realized that I did not carry enough cash to pay the bill. The neighbourhood grocer would not entertain any credit card of mine. He did not have an electronic card swipe machine! I made a quick look at my wallet. Knowing that there wasn't enough money to pay for all that I had picked, I started keeping away the items I did not immediately need. I made sure that I did not miss anything mentioned in the list to avoid any wrath, back home!

As I was doing this trade-off, the neighbourhood grocer understood my plight. He opened himself up gently to me and asked me if I had a problem. Before I could respond to him, he said, 'Gibson Sir, please take home whatever you want. You can pay me later'. I was stunned to hear my name from him. He knew that I worked for Shoppers Stop and he knew precisely in which apartment I lived! He told me he was acquainted with all my family members who were his regular customers. Believe me, this was the first time I visited that neighbourhood store. He had known me. He said that he had delivered products at my door. That day I realized the importance of customer relationship, truly forged by a well-intentioned small storeowner. His business, as he proved, was not only to know his products and service deliveries but also to know his customers like the back of his palm. Since then I have felt free to visit this store. Customer psychology is understood and practised by small storeowners quite well.

The shopkeeper's smile was the icebreaker and the sales transactions began. He had a ready smile for every customer who walked in! This made everyone welcome to his premises. Customer recognition is what the storeowner demonstrated! Despite his activity-filled busy hours of business, he made it a habit to acknowledge the presence of every customer. He demonstrated that true relationship is a matter of genuine concern for the customer. He understood the customer's plight first-hand and gave a ready solution. He did not want the customer to go disappointed because he did not have enough money, but offered to collect it from home. He showed that he trusted the customer! He reassured the customer that he could take home everything that he wanted and could pay later. A community retailer, serving a close circle of customers, he made every customer feel genuinely important.

An efficient retailer must know his customers accurately, and he must know as many of them as possible like the Cheap & Best store owner. Small retailers usually know their customers well as the customers may repeatedly come to the store. But in today's context of the store's catchment having many apartments in a single housing complex itself in a town, is it possible to know them all and remember their needs? It may only be possible to know some regular customers, although many customers might come often but not so frequently. It is very difficult to remember all of them in the current context of busy customer environments in retailing and to engage with everyone personally.

- How can we know all our customers? It is possible to know details of all the customers. If we have the POS solution, a simple billing system installed in the store, the software enables customer data capture. If the customer data is filled in then one can know all the purchase details of the customer. Once the data capture is done, even if the customer's telephone number alone is entered, all the details can be retrieved during the making of the new bill. The storeowner or manager can call up customers to get the order also. The address in the data may help in delivering messages, handbills, etc. during special occasions and promotions.

Footfalls

The importance of customers coming to a retail store is a no-brainer. Many customers come to the store every day. The store's daily sales are a function of the number of customers who visit the store and the quantum/value of goods each customer buys. By their gut feeling, the traditional retailers know how many customers come to the store each day and at what time the customer visits are highest during the day. Modern retailers count the customers who enter the store. It makes absolute business sense to count the customers who come to the store on a daily basis. Simple mechanical counters are available nowadays and one can easily keep a count of the number of customers visiting the store. Customer visits in simple term is known as 'footfalls'.

Conversion

All the customers who come to the store may not buy. Perhaps the merchandise needed by the customer may not be available in the store, or if the store is crowded and the customer thinks that it might take time to be served, he/she might go away without making a purchase. So, the number of customers buying at the store out of the number of customers who visit the store is known as 'conversion' rate, usually expressed in terms of percentage. The number of customers who have bought is directly calculated by the number of bills the store has raised that day with the assumption that each customer has bought in a single cash memo.

Ticket Size

The value of purchases made on a single bill is called the ticket size. The average ticket size for a store is calculated by dividing the day's sale value by the number of cash memos made that day. If the day's sales amount to ₹10,000 and 100 bills have been made, the average ticket size is ₹100.

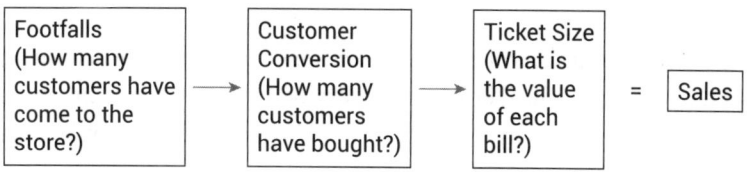

In the foregoing process,

- we can improve sales if we encourage more customers to visit the store.
- we can increase sales if we make all customers, who visit the store, buy goods unfailingly.
- we can increase the sales if we make customers buy more products.
- we can increase the sales if we sell value-added or higher value products and increase the ticket size.

Daily Footfalls	Conversion	Ticket Size (₹)	Daily Sales (₹)
100	80	200	16,000
100	90	200	18,000
120	110	200	22,000
100	80	250	20,000

Create compelling reasons for customers to visit the store.

- The right quality of products and the right price could always be the best reasons for the customers to visit your store.
- If we extend a courteous service, customers may like to visit our store.
- Encourage customers to leave the order so that we can door-deliver, which many new modern supermarkets do not do.
- Count footfalls so that we may take appropriate efforts to increase footfalls. If a husband and wife visit the store, we can take it as one customer unit.

Count the number of bills that are made in a day and compare them with the number of customers who have visited the store. Analyse reasons why customers went away without purchasing.

In a grocery store, if the conversion is less than 95 per cent, then it is a serious cause for concern.

- The store may not have the right products for the 5 per cent customers who didn't buy anything and the risk is that even the 95 per cent customers who purchased may not have purchased those products that were not in stock and, hence, they too may be dissatisfied. So, check for the out-of-stock items and arrange for replenishment immediately.
- If space for the customer to stand and buy is not adequate when the store is crowded, the customer may go away without buying. So, the speed of service is very important in achieving 100 per cent conversion.

To increase the ticket size:

- The store staff must sell as much and as many items as possible to the customer.
- Remind the customer of the items he/she may have forgotten.
- As many small stores are not in a free-access supermarket format, it may be very difficult for the customer to see all the products and, hence, the customer may not be instantaneously reminded of what he/she came to the supermarket for.
- Sell an item bigger or larger than the one the customer ordered. For example, if the customer orders half a kilogram of cashew nuts, convince him/her to buy 1 kg, highlighting the price advantage of buying a larger pack. There are many more ways of increasing the sales in-store and you may train sales people to do it effectively without fail with every customer.

While achieving the desired number of footfalls in the store is a result of good marketing efforts, achieving the right rate of conversion and the desired ticket size is the result of the efforts made within the retail store by the store people.

Understanding Customers Thoroughly: MSH Sarees Pvt. Ltd (Jashn Brand of Retail Stores), Mumbai

One can see the fashion-conscious Mr Chander Jashnani clad in smart formalwear often sporting suspenders that clasped his trousers. He has traversed the path of success in speciality retailing. That said, one should not forget that he has come up the hard way. Born as one of the nine children to his parents, he underwent his share of hardships in learning the tricks of the retail trade from his father. In the short spurts of time that he used to get from his father to spend with, he utilized them effectively to be with him and learn from him the nuances of how he dealt with his customers, his people and his suppliers. Mr Kundandas Jashnani, Mr Chander Jashnani's father moved from Larkama in Sindh after parting with his business during partition and opened a small department store in Nainital. He deployed his family business wisdom, and he did pretty well in his department store. Eventually, the department store concept weaned away as Mr Kundandas Jashnani gained expertise in the saree business. Among the various locations he visited from time to time to do business with customers, he found great potential in the city of Lucknow. He started a small saree shop in Lucknow in 1937. As he was progressing, he also relocated to Lucknow, now left with two stores to manage_one in Nainital and the other in Lucknow. He used to ponder about the similar stock mix that every store sold with respect to sarees in Lucknow.

Mr Kundandas Jashnani wanted to understand his customers better. He differentiated his store by identifying his customers as the 'class of the discerning modern woman' and offered exclusive merchandise that matched their tastes and preferences. He came to be quickly known for the range of premium silk sarees he sourced, stocked and sold. He called his store Modern Silk House. He positioned his store as an exclusive one for the design conscious even in those days when fashion and design were not taken seriously by the customers in a category like sarees. He made business connections with his clientele in the Samthars, Balrampurs, Tirwas, Singhais, Kasmandas, Kotwaras and the Nawabee families of Awadh. Mr Kundandas Jashnani travelled from place to place to source the right choices of the saree merchandise and often visited places like Kolkata and its suburbs to identify and develop specialized weavers to create exclusively for his store. There lay his skills of sourcing and getting the right sarees to sell. While other competing retailers sold the run-of-the-mill sarees, Mr Jashnani carved a special place for his store with his exclusive customer base.

Mr Chander Jashnani began to involve himself in the business by helping his father even when he was just 12 years of age. It was his passion to go to his father's store whenever he had free time. While his brothers too used to get involved in active selling behind the counters, Mr Chander Jashnani showed keen interest in travelling with his father and maternal uncle to visit suppliers and source sarees. He fondly remembers the time he spent with his father and the learning he gained from him as he cocreated designs with weavers and selected the right designs for the customers. He learnt the art of knowing the characteristics of each weave as he studied them from his father. He knew the right places for sourcing speciality sarees. The family as a whole worked together to make the store in Lucknow grow larger. As his brothers too shared the responsibility of running the stores by selling and extending customer service on the shop floor, Mr Chander Jashnani showed keen interest in travelling with his father, especially during holidays to source merchandise and make purchases for replenishing the sold merchandise and to introduce new designs on various occasions. Soon he became a good companion to his father on their purchase trips.

Mr Chander Jashnani completed his collegiate education in Lucknow and after that he was ready to begin his work full time in the Modern Silk House. His interest in saree buying made him undertake the sole responsibility of sourcing for the store full time and soon merchandising became his passion. He used to understand each design genre and source merchandise according to the needs of his customers. He even developed the art of taking orders from customers in advance and fulfilling them meticulously. The curiosity of every discerning customer used to be aroused by him as he chose to buy only one saree in every exclusive design to sell from the store. This paved the way for the happiness that every customer gained design exclusivity with her purchase. His father continued to guide him. When the time came for his father to take the back seat and retire from active travels in the early 1970s, Mr Chander Jashnani took over the reins of the key function of buying, and he became adept in understanding the tastes of the store's customers, although he continued to perform with his father's advice on design selection, sourcing and buying. The store space grew with every renovation and in 1993, the Modern Silk House in Lucknow became a three-level experiential saree store.

Mr Chander Jashnani understood from his father that there were three principles to follow while buying sarees efficiently:

Buy Outright: Mr Kundandas Jashnani always made outright purchases without availing any time from the vendor for making deferred payment for purchases. Mr Chander Jashnani learnt from his father that deferred payments could result in increase in prices by the suppliers and could push cost up considerably.

Negotiate Hard: The second principle that Mr Chander Jashnani learnt from his father is about hard negotiation of prices with the vendors. He learnt that he should not shy away from bargaining better prices from his vendors. If the shop owner's relationship with the vendor is good, he would often assume that the vendor would give the right prices, but he learnt from his father that further negotiation of prices with the vendors still worked well and brought down the cost of goods sold. He also learnt the art of finding the right prices by developing multiple vendors for similar saree categories, so that he could go to vendors who offered less prices and still negotiate with them.

Handpick Your Merchandise: Whatever he wanted for the store, Mr Kundandas Jashnani handpicked from the vendors by going through their collections in detail. Often vendors/manufacturers used to stock sarees in lots and would try to push to retailers what they had in stock. But Mr Kundandas Jashnani used to apply his understanding of customer tastes and buy the right ones by handpicking them. He never used to fall for the discounts offered on stock lots and carefully avoided unsuitable merchandise. This process paved the way for identifying the right merchandise for his customers and that was good enough learning for Mr Chander Jashnani to perfectly match the sarees sourced with customer tastes and preferences. Till today, Mr Chander Jashnani keeps in mind the aforementioned three principles he learnt from his father, and he has even taught his son Rahul Jashnani too to adopt the same principles as his policy.

The family business _Modern Silk House_ grew. The business witnessed allied diversification into retailing of the textile brand Raymond and similar businesses that were established by brothers in locations including Mumbai. Mr Chander Jashnani too wanted to branch out of his family business and start afresh in the year 2000. At that time, his son Rahul Jashnani had just completed his graduation in business studies from Houston and he was ready to help his father _ Mr Chander Jashnani. The father and son duo were mulling a number of allied ideas to hit upon a successful second innings. When they were visiting Mumbai for attending a retail conference, they happened to meet Mr Chandru Raheja of Shoppers Stop. Mr Jashnani had known about the success of Shoppers Stop as a department store business in India, and he had always dreamt of presenting his exclusive saree merchandise in large department stores like Shoppers Stop. This meeting became a boon for him when he casually mentioned to Mr Raheja that Shoppers Stop had the conspicuous gap of sarees in their merchandise and that he could put together a shop-in-shop there, given an opportunity. Soon the project was proposed and Mr Chander Jashnani came up with a brand name 'Jashn' to offer exclusive and designer sarees to the customers of Shoppers Stop in a shop-in-shop format. So, the first outlet opened in the New Delhi branch of Shoppers Stop, the very same year. In quick succession, Jashn opened its new business in most of the branches of the department store organization, opening doors in places such as Andheri, Bandra, Kandivali, Mulund, Ghatkopar in Mumbai and in Jaipur, *Gurgaon, Pune, Hyderabad, Chennai, Kolkata and so on. The flagship company of the father _ son team of Mr Chander and Rahul Jashnani has drawn its name from the summarized form of their surname, which also means celebration in Hindi. Mr Chander Jashnani opened an office and a warehouse subsequently in Raheja Vihar in Andheri, Mumbai, to enable timely supplies to all locations. Mr Jashnani was very particular about training the store staff in all the aspects of the merchandise and, thus, everyone employed in each shop-in-shop had the ability to sell well. He closely monitored the performance of each shop-in-shop on a daily basis and often he would return home only after midnight. His efforts did not stop there. He identified opportunities when the mall proliferation happened in India.

In 2003, Mr Chander Jashnani opened an exclusive Jashn store in R-Mall. Then he partnered with every good mall opening in India to have an exclusive brand store of Jashn there. The success of Jashn rode piggyback on the success of every mall. Today Jashn is a proud partner with every successful mall such as Inorbit, Phoenix, Forum and so on. Mr Chander Jashnani encouraged his son to go across borders. Present in more than 40 locations, spread in 21 cities in 45 company-owned and company-operated stores, Jashn has stores not only in India but also in two cities abroad, Dubai and Abu Dhabi. Mr Chander Jashnani is one example of an astute retailer who grabbed opportunities that lay amidst the burgeoning success of modern retailing in India and ride piggyback on it to achieve a celebrated success of his format!

Mr Chander Jashnani's reinvention strategy is to sell designer apparel at non-designer prices. He envisions to become an Indian multinational retail organization that would become the first name in ethnic, Indo-Western and lifestyle fashion while offering the contemporary woman exclusive Indian ethnic wear and fusion wear to make her look and feel great. Mr Chander Jashnani also wants to showcase the talents of Indian weavers and craftsmen to the world. He wants to set a record by being the most pervasively spread ethnic, fusion and lifestyle fashion wear retail chain soon not just in India but also in the world by 2020.

Key Takeaways from Jashn

- Understand customer needs thoroughly.
- Learn the ropes of the retail business by working on the retail floors since the beginning.
- Identify the success factors of the key function in the business you are responsible for.
- Bring about the right differentiation in the merchandise mix for your store to stand out uniquely to serve the right segment of customers.
- Establish relationship with as many customers as possible personally, by going out of your store premises and meeting them at their doorsteps.
- As you grow, move out of your comfort zone and relocate if necessary to spot new opportunities for growth.
- Sourcing the right merchandise at the right price should be your strength to win in retailing.
- Tweak your offering to suit the changing tastes and preferences of your new-generation customers.
- Keep updating technology applications in order to be available for your customers anytime, anywhere.

Organize Store Space Efficiently

SECRET 4

> Retail space is money. The retailer must focus on space productivity and calculate returns on space—that is, the revenue generated from every section of the shelf, display and signage areas.

Every retail store comes with limited space that needs to accommodate a definite quantity of stocks—both what is visible to the customers and what is tucked away in storage spaces. Though the store may be owned by the traditional retailer himself, there is a notional rental value that is incurred as part of the store's operating expenses. Others who take out a lease on the store pay a certain amount of rent for the store premises every month. The store space planning for a traditional retail store often centres around *space on hire* (the shelf space and show windows that suppliers and brand companies hire for a monthly rental in a retail store) given away to marketers for returns, and this planning begins with the exterior of the store.

The Sign Board

The signboard of the store is the sole indicator of the brand name of the store. Traditional retailers do not take this seriously and trade this space off to advertisers for paltry sums or more often free of cost in exchange to just get a painted façade. The advertiser occupies almost the whole signboard space with his own branding, leaving the store's brand to be seen in a miniscule proportion.

The signboard of the store should be prominently seen. Without interfering with the signboard, display boards to advertise key offerings from brands can always be put up from time to time for returns from brands and other service providers. Even though the neighbourhood may know your store well, it is relevant in the current competitive context for customers to readily see your store brand name and register the same in their minds.

Don't Trade Off Store Facade Signage Space to Advertise Other Brands

Find the Right Façade Spaces for Advertising

Exterior Spaces

Exterior spaces would include the other outside wall space and visible display counters. These counters can be used for the intending merchandising companies within the stock categories the store sells. These spaces could be planned for items of high margin the retailer wants to promote. The exterior spaces for hire should be given away with proper planning. In small towns, we often see all the walls of the store painted with advertiser's brands. Such spaces on hire should be given away for a period of time and not on a one-time basis as long as the life of the advertisement remains.

Interior Spaces

Often the traditional retailer does not understand the significance of store space utilization and frequently allows fast moving consumer goods suppliers and national brands to dictate the shelf space occupation under their own merchandising schemes and patterns. The store space is divided into four main areas:

- Display shelf space
- Floor stocking space
- Inside movement space
- Cash-till area

In many traditional retail stores unlike some modern supermarkets, space is usually very well utilized. The density of stocks is very high without any vacant spaces in both the display area and the stocking area. The movement area should just be enough for store people to move around and pick up things swiftly. The display of stocks in the planogram in a traditional retail store could be done with the fastest selling stocks in easy access so that service too is achieved faster. The most important point to ensure is the visibility of the whole store inside without any obstructions because in retailing, 'that which is seen is always sold'!

Planogram

The retailer needs to decide a planogram for his store, which is an array of merchandise display following a particular order on the linear shelf space, show windows and counters. It is a myth that only organized and modern stores such as supermarkets can have defined planograms, but a traditional retail store can have a very functional planogram too. Shelves can be allocated for merchandise categories and defined for eye-level vantage points and others so that space grading can be done for leasing out display space on hire. The planogram can be organized in such a way that *convenience products* such as biscuits and noodles are kept on the shelves, bulk grocery *staples* for selling in loose packs could be arranged in easy access for store staff handling, in the carpet floor space, and *impulse* items such as chocolates and lozenges can be kept near the cash counter.

Planogram

Adjacency Plan

Deciding what items have to be kept near one another in the shelves is known as an adjacency plan. A typical adjacency plan is built within the planogram discussed earlier, taking into consideration the adjacencies of product categories to be kept near each other. Food products are kept near each other—each brand near the other, and convenience categories like packaged non-food non-toxic products are chosen to be placed near each other. Household sanitation and pest control products have to be kept away from food products and they may be kept near surfactants and detergents. Traditional retailers usually follow this rationale as a common practice.

Rent Fixation Methodology for Space on Hire

Currently, traditional retailers do not follow any methodology for leasing out shelf display space on hire. It is only decided by FMCG companies and national brands based on the quantum of purchase made by the retailer. Suppliers always decide the display value not based on the product exposure to the customers' eyeballs but the sales of their products. This ultimately amounts to pressurizing the retailer to buy quantities which match the supplier's offer made under the banner of display.

The rent fixation for the space on hire should be in proportion to the going rental per square foot per month of retail space of that shopping area. For example, if the going rent is ₹100 per square foot per month, the linear shelf space rental proportion at eye-level vantage point could be calculated at five times the rental value. Therefore, the rate per square foot of shelf space on hire per month is ₹500 per square foot per month. For other less significant display spaces, the retailer and the supplier could decide the proportion of linear shelf space on hire mutually.

- Never give away all your signboard space for others to advertise for the favour of getting your signboard painted or for a one-time fee.
- Offer the extra space above, below or around your signboard on hire. Always charge for a period of three months or six months on contract.
- Calculate the space on hire in multiples of the current rent per square foot in the area.
- Recommended shelf space on hire = five times the rental value per square foot
  - If the lease rental in the shopping area is ₹100 per square foot and the shelf space on hire taken by a product/brand is 10 square feet, then the retailer should charge 10 × 100 × 5 = ₹5,000 per month.

    (The brand/product suppliers try to link shelf-on-hire charges to the retailer's purchases over a period of time, but as a retailer, one has to check the hire charges offer to match five times the value of the lease rental—actual or notional.)
- Recommended signboard space on hire = 10 times the store space rental value per square foot (or the cost of monthly lease value per square foot of hoardings in the city or town if applicable)
  - If the lease rental in the shopping area is ₹100 per square foot and the façade signage space on hire taken by a product/brand is 10 square feet, then the retailer should charge 10 × 100 × 10 = ₹10,000 per month, ₹30,000 for 3 months and ₹60,000 for 6 months.
  - Alternatively, the signboard space on hire may be charged on the value of the ongoing billboard rents in the area. For example, the rent per month of a billboard (known as hoarding also) of 20' × 10' (200 square feet) is ₹50,000 per month, which works out to ₹250 per square foot. So, for a 10 square feet facade signage space on hire, the monthly rent could work out to ₹2,500.

Measuring Store Space Performance

The space utilization in a store is measured usually by the value of sales achieved per square foot, which is called sales per square foot. If the day's sale in the store is ₹10,000 and the total square feet of the store for which rent is paid is 100, then 10,000/100 = 100, that is ₹100 per square foot per day. The same can be calculated for a month also when the month's sale value is divided by the total square feet area. That means if the monthly sale is ₹300,000, then 300,000/100 = 3,000, that is ₹3,000 per square foot per month. The same formula can be applied to gross margin (gross profit) also and one can calculate the gross margin per square foot for the store, which is known as Gross Margin Return on Footage (GMROF). Similarly, shelf display income also can be calculated for every square foot of shelf space given away on hire called Space on Hire Income on Footage (SOHIOF).

Space Hygiene

The retailer has to ensure proper store hygiene. Appropriate fumigation should be carried out to keep off pests and unnecessary odour. Fumigation must be done periodically following the norms of an authorized pet-control company and care should be taken to secure food products from any direct contact with pest-repellent, rodent trap and fumigation materials. Small retailers get on usually with the daily routine of their work and tend to neglect the cleanliness of the space inside the store. Proper care ought to be taken to keep the store in neat array and in perfect cleanliness. Bad odour can drive away customers and at the same time it can invite pests that may destroy goods as well.

Important Points to Consider in Store Space Management

1. Utilize store space up to 100 per cent with high density of display and stocking.

2. Ensure that store brand signage is prominently put up and is visible to build the store brand.
3. Plan display spaces—both in the exterior and the interiors—well.
4. Define rates for space on hire prudently.
5. Measure sales per square foot per month for the store and monitor space performance.
6. See that proper store ventilation as well as pest control and management is comprehensively done.

Scaling Up from a Sidewalk Hawking Space: A. P. Mani & Sons, Mumbai

It was not just a humble beginning for Nagesh Nadar of A. P. Mani & Sons, but a beginning from scratch, literally. He started as a sidewalk street vendor selling vegetables in Chembur, Mumbai, in 1982. He recalls how he came to Mumbai from Alwarthirunagari in Tuticorin district 30 years ago and started hawking by the side street in Chembur with an investment of only ₹1.25. He had just passed his 6th standard examination, and with no further interest in studies but with just the zeal to win in life, he had come to Mumbai.

Nagesh says with happiness, 'I could win many loyal customers for my sidewalk spread of vegetables'. Yes, he began retailing vegetables as a hawker. Three years later, in 1985, he could afford to set up a small 4' × 4' leased petty shop to retail his merchandise. His brother, Suresh Nadar, too joined the business having passed his 8th standard in Mumbai. Nagesh says that he moved his whole family to Mumbai. He says, 'My mother, Arasi Ammal, has been a great support and inspiration to me. My business has been the sole source of income for my whole family'.

He says with pride that he put up a signboard, 'A. P. Mani & Sons', on the small shop named after his father A. P. Mani. Nagesh expanded his retailing space gradually. Today, A. P. Mani & Sons has grown into a supermarket spread over 2,000 square feet of Nagesh's own retailing space in Chembur where he moved into in 2003.

The strategy for growth, as Nagesh avers, is his understanding of specific consumer needs. Right from the beginning, his customers who have been mostly working women would alight from trains and walk up to his shop to buy vegetables, as they would go back home. Nagesh began to add value to them by giving them good quality vegetables often cut and packed for their convenience. He recalls his trials of value addition to customer convenience. As an example, he cites the way he used to pack and deliver vegetables and fruits for every customer. Nagesh says,

> In the earlier days, all the vegetables a customer bought would be dumped into one big paper bag and handed over to the customer. I saw that the customers were not too happy with the way I delivered the goods as they had to spend time to separate every kind of vegetable from the other in the mixed bag, which was a cumbersome process. Later, I packed each kind of vegetable in a newspaper wrap and delivered such multiple wraps into one paper bag. Still I found that customers were unhappy as the packs when kept in refrigerators became soggy and my customers had to repack each kind of vegetable in various containers at home to store in refrigerators.

He says that in the mid-1990s, he saw the penetration of refrigerators into each of his customers' homes in Mumbai. 'I began to pack each variety of vegetable in a separate food grade plastic cover and then deliver to customers so that they could store them straight in their refrigerators with ease', he says. The strategy of selling pre-cut and pre-packed vegetables with the ultimate customer convenience in mind, paid off. Nagesh says that he knew from experience how much quantity of each variety the customers would buy. Lesser weight packs of spices such as ginger and chilli and more packs of vegetables and still more packs of onions and potatoes! He expanded his product categories largely with A. P. Mani's private labels and own packaging of staples and snacks.

As new supermarkets opened up, Nagesh struck an alliance with Haiko Supermarket in Powai, Mumbai, to supply the store's needs of vegetables and fruits. His convenience pre-cut packs became a big hit with customers. A. P. Mani & Sons Vegetables and Fruits (P) Ltd has been a pioneering vendor with Haiko Supermarket. Nagesh is one of the first small retailers to identify the needs of the emerging modern trade and to play a significant role by becoming one of its key suppliers. He also supplies A. P. Mani branded snacks to many retailers. He says, 'This new business of collaboration I developed with Haiko, stands us in good stead as a supplier to a large retailer'.

The other main strength that Nagesh developed was procurement. He says that even today he wakes up early in the morning and goes to the Vashi wholesale 'mandi' to have hands-on knowledge of all the goods and their pricing. He has a commission 'mandi' operating from the Vashi market as well. Controlling wastage is a key aspect of his business, he says. Nagesh says that good quantity management based on knowledge and experience is the key to control 'dump' in vegetable and fruits retailing.

He attributes his success to his vision of having his own independent building that could house his business offices under one roof soon. He says that hard work and self-confidence have taken A. P. Mani & Sons to what it is today ₹300 million per annum business with more than 150 people directly employed. Nagesh says with pride, 'Many educated and trained people now support me in my organization'. Strong will power is another key aspect, he says, that motivated him and his family. Nagesh had a polio attack during his childhood and is limp in his right leg, that was fractured, too, recently, adding further injury, but he says, 'I am never limp in my heart or mind', and that positive attitude drives him to achieve growth.

Nagesh says that his strength still lies in successfully managing small vegetable and grocery retail formats. He opened the first A. P. Mani Sasta Bazaar in about 335 square feet in Brindavan, Thane, in January 2013. 'This', he says, 'is the first of the 25 such small format stores planned to be opened in Mumbai in the next three years'. He reels off the plan with details from his mind and mentions that he is guiding the next generation that is getting ready to support him in the expansion of his business, post their studies.

Speaking of the hurdles to growth, he cites his own lack of education as the prime impediment. He says, from his experience, that he had to face difficulties and overcome communication issues with suppliers, banks and other stakeholder companies because he was not sufficiently educated. The next aspect he mentions, when it comes to an impediment to growth, is lack of effective fund management. He says that managing day-to-day cash flows is important in small retail business. 'Planning and controlling expenses along with wise margin management can propel growth in business', he says. Nagesh believes that banks could play a major role in helping small retailers with the required funds for growth. He also says that business has to be brought to books at the earliest, and if the small retailer pays taxes to the government properly, he can start climbing the ladder of growth. The next aspect that he emphasizes for growth in small business is the relationship with suppliers. According to Nagesh, a good relationship with all the suppliers can take one's retail business to greater heights, especially by handholding the business not only by the extension of credit but also by timely supplies. Then he says, 'The other major factor that brings growth to my business is the people in my retail business. My people always stand by me through thick and thin'. As our conversation was drawing well beyond lunchtime, he excused himself promptly to remind someone over phone to order food for his driver, as he was preparing to take him to his next destination, and that showed Nagesh's concern for his people!

He says that family unity is of great importance for the growth of the small retail business, and he always includes his whole family when it comes to remembering the people behind his growth _ his mother, brother and the whole family. His children and his brother's children are studying. His first son, Arul Prashant, has just finished his Master of Business Administration, and he has already got on his training stint to support his father and uncle. Nagesh tells them, 'We are working tirelessly every day and you may support us in our weak areas'.

He has a simple philosophy that India is a vast place and there is room for all. He says, 'People will sell coffee beverage for ₹3 and also for ₹300 and specific buyers will be there for both. So, why should anyone be worried about any competition?'

Key Takeaways from A. P. Mani & Sons

- Work hard with self-confidence even as you begin in a small space, in a small way.
- Identify real customer needs and add value.
- Always take care to be with your customers, bank, suppliers and people.
- Have ideas and work on them even if you do not have big money.
- Put your vision in place.
- Bring your business to books and pay taxes. These are the first rungs of the ladder of your business growth.
- Take the support of the family, especially the younger generation. They would fill in for your weak areas and make the business robust.

Stock up the Store for Profit

SECRET 5

[*Deciding the quantity of merchandise to hold optimally in the right stock density in every part of the store to sell the maximum stocks is significant to achieve the desired profitability.*]

The retailer can achieve more profits if the merchandise in the store is managed efficiently. While planning the inventory holding for a retail store one needs to consider the achievement of the following seven 'rights':

The *Right Product,* in the *Right Quantity,* in the *Right Quality,* in the *Right Mix and Assortment,* at the *Right Price,* in the *Right Place* and in the *Right Time.*

In a retail store, the right products have to be kept in the right places, in the right quantity, in the right quality, in the right mix and assortment, at the right price and in the right time. Timeliness refers to the seasonality of product demand, and such seasons and sales of products during seasons have to be well understood by the retailer.

The quantity of stocks to hold in a retail store to sell is very important to achieve profitability. One can do business with whatever amount of stocks one can buy to sell. But there has to be a limit defined to the quantity of stocks to be held in the store. This limit is a function of the space available in the store to stock and display, and more importantly, it is a function of sales.

So, if the sales quantities are foreseen properly, then just-in-time purchases can be made. In a small store, though it is easier for the owner or manager to know from memory what sells more and how fast, it may be difficult to actually know the rate of sales of all the products in stock. Often, it is only 20 per cent of the total stocks that may account for 80 per cent of the store's sale. It is, thus, important for the retailer to understand the rate of stock turn of each item and each category of merchandise so that buying efficiencies can be achieved, spoilage can be prevented and more profits can be made. For example, suppose a retailer has ₹100,000 worth of stocks on an average at any given point in time (so, his investment in merchandise is ₹100,000), and he usually takes one month to sell ₹100,000 value of merchandise and makes a gross margin (gross profit) of ₹20,000. If the retailer takes efforts and sells ₹100,000 value within 20 days with the same value of stocks, he now makes a gross profit of ₹20,000 in 20 days and if he sells at the same rate, he gets a profit of ₹30,000 in a month. This is known as Gross Margin Return on Inventory (GMROI).

Stock turn: It is the number of times the stocks are rotated in a store, which is known by the rate of sales made out of the quantity of stocks held in the store. For example, if the sales value of the store per day is ₹10,000 and the total stock value is ₹100,000, then the percentage of sales from stock is 10 per cent (100,000/10,000). So, it will take 10 days to sell the whole store's stock. Hence, the stock turn rate is 3 times a month or 36 times a year. If the stock is reduced to ₹75,000, then the whole store's stock can be sold in 7.5 days and the stock turn per month will be 4 (30/7.5) times and it will be 48 times per annum. In the same scenario, if the sales value is increased to ₹12,500 per day and the stock value is ₹100,000, then it takes 8 days to sell the whole store's stocks and the stock turn per month will be 3.75 times. The annual stock turn will be 45 times. Stock turn is always expressed in number of times. This can also be calculated on the quantity of stocks. Stock turn can be calculated for a product item, for a category and for a store as well.

Stock turn Scenario 1: If the sale is ₹10,000 per day and the average stock value is ₹100,000

$$\% \text{ of sale from stock} = \frac{\text{Sale}}{\text{stock}} \times 100$$

$$= \frac{10,000}{10,0000} \times 100 = 10\%$$

To sell 10% of the stock, it takes = 1 day
So, to sell 100% of the stock it takes = 10 days

$$\text{Stock turn/year} = \frac{365 \text{ days}}{10 \text{ days}} = 36.5 \text{ times in a year}$$

$$\text{Stock turn/month} = \frac{30 \text{ days}}{10 \text{ days}} = 3 \text{ times in a month}$$

Stock turn Scenario 2: If the sale is ₹10,000 per day and the average stock value is reduced to ₹75,000

$$\% \text{ of sale from stock} = \frac{\text{Sale}}{\text{stock}} \times 100$$

$$= \frac{10,000}{75,000} \times 100 = 13.3\%$$

To sell 13.3% of stock, it takes 1 day
So to sell 100% of stocks = 7.5 days

$$\text{Stock turn/year} = \frac{365 \text{ days}}{7.5 \text{ days}} = 48.7 \text{ times in a year}$$

$$\text{Stock turn/Month} = \frac{30 \text{ days}}{7.5 \text{ days}} = 4 \text{ times in a month}$$

GMROI_Scenario 1: If the shop's stock value is ₹100,000 and if it takes 10 days to sell the whole stock at the rate of sales of ₹10,000 per day, then the stock turn achieved will be 3 times in a month. If the profit is 20 per cent, the total amount of profit achieved for the month will be ₹60,000.

$$\text{GMROI} = \text{Sales for the period} \times \text{Stock turn} \times 20 \text{ per cent}$$
$$= 100{,}000 \times 3 \times 20\% = ₹60{,}000 \text{ per month}$$

GMROI_Scenario 2: If the shop's stock value is the same as Scenario 1, that is, ₹100,000, the gross margin (gross profit) remains the same at 20 per cent, but the whole stock is sold within a period of 7.5 days instead of the 10 days in Scenario 1, then the daily sale increases to ₹13,333. In this scenario with the same stock level and increased rate of sales, the profit achieved for the month increases to ₹80,000.

$$\text{GMROI} = \text{Sales for the period} \times \text{Stock turn} \times 20\%$$
$$= 100{,}000 \times 4 \times 20\% = ₹80{,}000 \text{ per month}$$

The difference between Scenario 1 and Scenario 2 is an increase of ₹20,000 gross profit per month in Scenario 2 because of the increased rate of sales and reduced stock holding time, given the total sale being the same. The stock turn and GMROI can be calculated for a product SKU or for a category of products taking into consideration the sales/stock/gross margin figures of the product or category and one can identify for correction and taking appropriate actions on those products that fall below the store's average stock turn or GMROI.

Prudent Buying: If a retailer buys fresh vegetables to sell, he ought to predict the day's sale and then buy. Perishable items like vegetables have to be sold within the day. The retailer may discount prices by the end of the day gradually to clear perishables so that the un-saleable remains to be dumped are limited and losses are contained. Items such as potatoes, carrots and onions may stay fresh for a few days more, and purchasing of these items can be made in bulk to last for, say, three days so that such buying scale can get the retailer more margins.

Many goods supplied by national brands, FMCG and distributors are often delivered through an order booked by the distributors and suppliers. Each FMCG company may try to 'oversell' to the retailer in order to occupy maximum shelf space in the category in the store by offering purchase linked schemes, offers (the suppliers call them quantity purchase schemes, trade load offers, etc.) and above all, by extending credit. The retailer has to be very careful to understand how many days the stocks may last and if stocks are over-bought then the stock turn will be affected. If the stock turn is affected, the store's profit is affected. Risk of stock shrinkage (the phenomenon of loss of stocks or quantity loss in the store resulting in losses for the store due to various reasons—reasons of merchandise quality loss, quantity reduction, wastage, pilferage, shop-lifting, etc.) is more if the stocks are going to be on the shelves for a long time without selling. So, there is always a tie between the suppliers and the retailers—while the suppliers want to sell more and more to drive the stock balance in their favour, the retailer orders the right quantities bargaining for the maximum schemes and offers.

Don't buy stocks arbitrarily. Know your inventory and sales rate before making purchase of each item for the store.

The retailer, hence, has to know thoroughly what sells well in what quantities and when. This is difficult for the retailer to know offhand in the current scenario where the number of SKUs of merchandise items has gone very high with many products being manufactured, imported, distributed and sold by companies that are wanted and used by customers too. In earlier days, the number of SKUs in a small store were perhaps around 500 or even less, but today in the same-sized store it may be 5,000 or even more. To remember the sale rate of 5,000 SKUs is practically impossible for a normal human being. So, if a system like the POS with the capability to generate sales and stock management reports is in place, one can easily know the current and desired stock turn rate, the present stock in hand and then order accordingly.

Merchandise Hierarchy and SKU: The merchandise in the store can be grouped and clustered for a good understanding of sale and stock management. The store merchandise can be largely classified into departments such as food, wash care, skin care, stationery and household products. Under food, the retailer can bring categories such as grocery, packaged food, fresh vegetables and meat and poultry. Further a category like packaged food can have sub-categories such as biscuits, noodles and so on. Under biscuits, the classification of brands such as Britannia, Parle and Sunfeast can be done. Say, under Britannia, Milk Bikis 25 g pouch, 100 g, 200 g, are included and the variant option of 25 g is an SKU, the variant option of 100 g is another SKU, the variant option of 150 g is another SKU and the variant option of 200 g is yet another SKU.

Department	:	Food
Categories	:	Packaged Food, Fresh Food, Staples, etc.
Brands	:	Britannia, Parle, ITC Sunfeast, etc.
Sub-brand Options	:	Milk Bikis, Good Day, Tiger, etc.
Stock Keeping Unit 1, 2, 3	:	25 g 100 g 150 g 200 g

This hierarchical clustering concept is called merchandise hierarchy and this helps the retailer decide how many brands to keep in the store and what SKUs to sell from the store. This helps in understanding from the system which category, which brand and which options and which SKUs sell more in the store and what stocks are not selling too. From this the retailer can learn which ones are the top 50 selling SKUs in the store and which ones are the slow sellers in the store. This can help the retailer order stocks carefully and avoid losses. A small retail store should restrict the number of items it sells under a category to carefully control inventory and achieve the best sales too. The merchandise hierarchy is a tool to maintain discipline in inventory planning, control and buying without allowing suppliers to dump stocks in the store.

Ten Ways to Increase Gross Margins

1. Bargain with brands and suppliers for more margins, schemes and offers.
2. Display the products and brands that give maximum margins in the category. Identify them SKU-wise and display at eye-level in the planogram. Recommend and sell to customers.
3. Repack bulk products such as grocery and grains and develop your own private labels. Pack them in your own store-branded bags. This will not only give the retailer more margins and profit but will enable the retailer build his own store brand gradually.
4. Try and make your own snack products. It is quite easy to make chips and domestic snacks in a back-end kitchen and brand them with your store brand name.
5. Popular branded beverages give considerably good extra percentage margin on terms of exclusivity under the condition that the retailer will not sell a competing brand. This

call needs to be taken carefully because if customer needs are not met, the customer may not come back to the store.
6. In the case of saleable merchandise, the retailer may be confident to forge a tie-up with a supplier or brand on pre-committed quantities for extra percentage of margins.
7. Analyse every category for its top 20 brands/SKUs that give maximum margins to the store and see that you promote them with your own displays.
8. Buy products such as fresh vegetables and fruits from wholesale markets along with 10 or 20 other nearby retailers forming a group so that big quantities of purchase can yield a minimum 2 per cent more profit on such fast-moving fresh products.
9. Train every staff to do upselling (suggest more quantity or a larger pack to the customer) and cross-selling (if a customer buys bread, ask whether he would need to buy eggs and sell to the customer) to each customer without fail.
10. Use a **POS** billing system that can give you reports on sales, stock and margins of even each SKU and monitor margin performance regularly.

Repack and Label Products with Store Brand Name

Strategic Game Plan: It is said that a bundle of sticks is always stronger than a single stick and if MSME are divided among themselves, they'll be no stronger than a single stick. A bundled or group work strategy for MSME can bring great results. It is indeed difficult to come together to form cohesively working groups and if all MSME come together to do it they'll gain a good deal of competitive advantage. Though difficult, the retailers in every town, big or small, can come together in groups and the current MSME/merchants and shopkeepers' associations should facilitate the formation of groups to network and function together with clearly defined responsibilities.

Retailer Category	Strategy	Action Plan
Small Retailers	Ant-clump Strategy	• Form a closely working network as horizontal strategic groups • Group bulk buying of products to gain margin advantages • Share defined sourcing responsibilities • Create alliances with wholesale markets and suppliers to gain scale in sourcing • Use common supply chain resources for transporting goods to save costs
Medium-sized retailers	Soldering Strategy	• Forge a horizontal strategic approach and form chains of membership outlets • Focus on catchment consumer needs • Wide coverage of members over a city or a region • Vertical strategic alliances facilitated by co-operative movement of retailers • Invest in private label manufacturing, packaging and distribution • Use cloud-based common IT system for just-in-time merchandise replenishments

Ant-clump Strategy: Fire ants enhance their efficiency by being together in a group. They can form a clump to fight odds and can even form the shape of a raft to stay afloat during floods for months. Small retailers in every town can form networks and do co-operative buying. Such bulk buying can be done directly from wholesale markets to gain distinct price advantages. Local networking to buy in bulk can work well for various food items, staples and fresh categories. Such bulk buying and distributing among members in the network will have the benefit of cost reduction in transportation and obtaining discounts on bulk buying. Retailers may join together and share defined sourcing and distribution responsibilities among themselves. When price advantage as a result of bulk buying is obtained, buying becomes extremely efficient. Common distribution can help in cost reduction as many small retailers could share expenses. In small towns such co-operatively networked sourcing can be done on staple and locally sourced products and it can extend to other categories and even to the extent of bargaining for more margins from distributors of brands and FMCG products too.

Soldering Strategy: Medium-sized retailers in India can, in addition, enter into more organized co-operative efforts such as setting up common manufacturing and distribution facilities for products like snack food items and others that could form a common private label strategy for a group of retailers. Such a co-operative manufacturing, packaging, branding and distribution effort will provide a good deal of additional margins to retailers. Besides, if quality is maintained well, as the availability of such co-operatively manufactured products and in-store private label categories will be only among the member retailers, it becomes a compellingly differentiated merchandise proposition that can bring captive customers to the member stores. The retailers may make investments for co-operative manufacturing and distribution among themselves. The manufacturing and distribution entity could function as a co-operative society with the participating member retailers. A common cloud-based Information Technology (IT) and System services can also connect the co-operative group and enable faster and easy replenishments.

A retail store becomes profitable only if the merchandising plan and buying are efficient. Prudent co-operative practices and carrying out a well-defined plan in buying and maintaining stocks well can only render fresh products at the right prices to consumers.

Right Product Strategies: Patanjali Ayurved Limited, Haridwar

Patanjali_the very name brings to mind instantly the big brand of natural and ayurvedic products that leapt to meteoric popularity in India in the recent times. Baba Ramdev, a yoga exponent and meditation guru cofounded the organization Patanjali Ayurved Limited, in 2006 along with Acharya Balkrishna, a partner of Baba with the same roots in yoga and Ayurveda. Acharya Balkrishna has to his credit many patents in ayurveda and related research. With the sole objective of propagating the goodness of natural, herbal and ayurvedic products to the consuming masses of India, both the swamis established the company.

Baba Ramdev has been a popular yoga guru in India. Acharya Balkrishna leveraged the goodness, thus, propagated and used his research and ayurvedic talents to create a plethora of products that could be commercially marketed. Patanjali is a name quite significant and relevant to the business proposition, as it has been taken after Patanjali, who wrote the yogic guidelines many centuries ago.

Acharya Balkrishna was quick to develop an array of products under the Patanjali brand_ayurvedic, herbal and natural. When many organizations, even with their boastful infrastructure and research and development facilities, themselves have been struggling to develop new products, Acharya Balkrishna's in-depth knowledge of the science of ayurveda helped him zero in on a range of relevant products to cater to the current needs of customers, at large. He developed a range of natural food products, ayurvedic preparations, herbal products, etc., which were readily sampled by customers, and trials were induced on a large scale to enable them to buy the products. The company established a network of distributors, many of whom are the ardent followers of Baba. Patanjali products found a good deal of space not only on the shelves of multitudes of retailers but also on the minds of millions of customers! Patanjali brand of products carved a niche for itself in an enviable measure both in the FMCG segment in India and in the uniquely growing natural and organic health segment. Acharya Balkrishna focused largely on the distribution of the products he uniquely developed, to every nook and corner of India. This helped the brand notch up a large turnover to the said tune of ₹100 billion in the financial year 2016_2017. What took almost half a century for many multinational companies, it took only a decade for Acharya Balkrishna to take Patanjali to its current stature. With over 25 categories and more than 500 SKUs in its product range portfolio, Patanjali as a brand gives a run for their money to established brands such as Maggi, Head & Shoulders, Pears and many more.

The three-dimensional strategy that Acharya Balkrishna hit upon and adopted for reaching consumers, combines the following:

1. A traditional distribution network consisting of distributors and millions of retailers.
2. A key account retail network collaborating with many organized retailers such as Big Bazaar, Star Bazaar, Reliance Mart, Easyday, Spencer's, Hypercity and many other hypermarkets and supermarkets.
3. A chain of Patanjali brand of retail stores.

Though Acharya Balkrishna initially focused on his distribution network and key account distribution, he entered into own store retailing only since 2010. Since then this alternative distribution strategy has resulted in becoming the brand's mainstay. The brand's penetration into smaller towns is phenomenal with the help of its own store retail channel. Acharya Balkrishna cocreated several entrepreneurs by way of franchising its brand of retail stores. These stores are said to be currently around 5,000 across India. Again, as many retailers struggle to populate their stores in many locations, Acharya Balkrishna is seen to have done it in full-throttled ease. He also launched around 12 mega retail stores, operating in the metros of India. Whenever a new store is established to cover a new market, Patanjali initiates trial consumption through extensive sampling of its products. Every retail store performs the additional role of being an ayurvedic advisory centre besides retailing its products. There are three kinds of retail formats Patanjali establishes_ Patanjali Chikitsalaya, which is a clinic with ayurvedic doctors, Patanjali Arogya Kendra, which is a health and wellness centre and Swadeshi Kendra which is a non-medicine product store. Run by entrepreneurs who are franchisees, Patanjali trains its retail people in ayurveda and certifies them as ayurvedic medical practitioners. Free consultation is offered in these retail stores and such a service ensures a huge amount of footfalls that then get converted to sales.

The availability of a whole range of products for healthy consumption, healing and natural nutrition coupled with free consultation form a big conceptual strength to ensure the success of every Patanjali retail store. FMCG brands, however big they may be, in India do not venture into retailing products through their own brand stores for the obvious reason of inadequacy of a wide enough range required to make a retail planogram for viability. Acharya Balkrishna has succeeded in creating a large enough range of products offered with related services to satisfy a wide spectrum of customer profiles.

Franchisees who operate Patanjali stores are chosen by dint of their keenness and interest in such natural, herbal and ayurvedic benefits along with the franchisee's capability to invest to run the retail store successfully. The brand supports franchisees efficiently with intense training on products and consultation services periodically. While the mega stores are spread over an area of over 2,000 square feet each, the typical Patanjali franchised store area ranges from 200 to 400 square feet. The smallest store could even be set up with a humble investment of ₹50,000 while the bigger ones would need investment anywhere between ₹100,000 and ₹200,000. Seeing its meteoric growth, Acharya Balkrishna has established multiple manufacturing units to meet the ever-growing demand from consumers. He has also set up a large Food and Herbal Park in Haridwar under the food park scheme of the Government of India. Plans are afoot to set up many more units in the other parts of the country to sustain the brand's growth.

Patanjali is fast expanding its retail presence to cover even very small towns in the country. Acharya Balkrishna is said to have set a target of 100,000 retail stores to be established in India soon to achieve the status of having the largest retail footprint in India in a record time! Aiming to be the world's largest FMCG company is by no means a small target but it seems to be within an arm's reach for both Baba Ramdev and Acharya Balkrishna to achieve, within a few years from now.

Key Takeaways from Patanjali

- Every entrepreneur can make one's own inherent ideas and capabilities work effectively.

- When one understands one's strengths thoroughly, one can use them to overcome any kind of challenges.

- A noble objective of serving the social cause of propagating a healthy life to the masses could result in new business opportunities. An entrepreneur could be successful when he looks to fulfil a social purpose through his business ultimately.

- Commercialization of a whole new concept successfully, is possible when one puts his heart and soul into it.

- Effective partnering with those who share in one's vision, would enable the achievement of complete business success.

- Genuine service that adds value to the customer, if combined with the selling of products can go a long way to meet with success.

- Bask not on your laurels of success but continue to serve the community through the expansion of your business in new territories worldwide seeking to become the largest.

Optimize Store Operations

SECRET 6

[*The crux of store operations is all about following defined processes for efficiently serving customers every time, keeping store expenses as low as possible, always.*]

A retailer's responsibility is to operate the store smoothly. There are a few functional areas of store operations that a retailer needs to focus on, in order to run the store without any hindrances.

Register under the Required Store Licences

A retail store in India needs to be registered under mandatory licences and permissions. The most important thing to do is the registration of the store under the Shops & Establishments Act and Sales Tax. Almost every state enables shops and establishments to download the necessary forms from its website for registration and also guides the whole registration process. The act governs the shop's operating hours as well as labour regulations with restriction on the employment of child labour (no child below 12 years of age can be employed in any retail store). Exemptions for opening the store on holidays can be obtained from the authorities.

If the retail store prepares and sells food, then the storeowner has to apply for Food Safety and Standards Authority of India (FSSAI) licence. The licensing processes in India have now been so simplified that the retailer can himself approach the municipal or corporation authorities, who will guide them on obtaining the required health and other licences in case of food retailing.

Define Sales Target

Plan a daily target to achieve in the store and share the same with all the employees so that everyone as a team will make a concerted effort to sell in order to achieve the common goal. Then everyone will work on seeing to it that the right products are stocked and sold well. Many owners try to keep the sales figures in small retail stores a secret for fear that the sales value might become known to everybody. Many small retailers have overcome this fear and those with a shared vision specifying targets for the day and goals for the month clearly can perform and win.

Customer Service

A retail store must ensure prompt service to customers. As there may be restricted space in a small store for customers even to stand and order during busy hours, every member of staff must act swiftly to serve customers. Each member of the staff must take charge of a customer or a few customers at the same time and serve them well and serve fast as well. An effective POS billing system can ensure fast billing so that customers are served accurately as well. Queues at the cash tills of large stores during busy days of shopping put customer off, and small stores can compete effectively by delivering much faster service to customers both at the store and at the door as well.

Stock Receipts and Maintenance

The major role of store operations is to receive all the stocks properly when they arrive in the store. If the stocks could be entered into the system, they can be easily monitored. The shelves have to be attended to every day for cleaning and replenishing the stocks. This responsibility should be divided and given to each sales staff in the store for proper monitoring. The planogram, as we discussed in the space management chapter, must be maintained in order to define the exact number of pieces of each item on display on the shelves if possible so that one may find out in a jiffy what has been sold from the store. Stock taking also becomes easier if the products are arranged on the shelves in a definite number in display. The shelves can be arranged in a visually appealing manner along with 'shelf-talkers' to announce offers and deals to the customers. Visual merchandising is the art of presenting products in an attractive manner to appeal to the customers.

Receive and Account Stocks When They Arrive in the Store

Shrinkage or Stock Loss Prevention

Proper care must be taken to avoid stock losses. Check whether all the packs are intact and especially whether own-store private label products are packed in good quality materials. Identify products with manufacturing and packing defects and return them to suppliers and distributors regularly. Identify products with closer expiry dates and try to sell them faster with discounts and markdowns. Eliminate expired products from shelves regularly and return them to suppliers as per agreed terms or destroy them. Train store people to secure products from shoplifting. Close-circuit TV surveillance has become much cheaper to install and once people know that the store is under surveillance, it will deter many from stealing.

Keep Store Operating Expenses Low

Those that usually top the list of all store-operating expenses are the rental cost (often expressed as occupancy cost which is calculated as a total of interest on rental deposits if any, Service Tax, on rent, etc. along with rental) and employment cost (employment cost includes salaries, employee welfare expenses and other benefits, if any). Other expenses include the store running expenses such as electricity consumption charges, telephone charges, travel and communication expenses, sales promotion and marketing expenses, supply expenses and so on. Each of these expenses could be measured as a percentage to sales turnover every month so that the retailer can understand and identify where expense is going high so that it could be contained.

Manage Store People Well

Train store people in actual selling by detailing out how to greet the customer within a few seconds of the customer's arrival, how to wear a natural smile always, how to be dressed well, how to speak to customers, how to upsell and cross-sell, how to attend to them and recommend an alternative product if the one the customer has asked for is not available, etc. Continuous on-the-job improvement interventions for sales staff must be done by the storeowner, manager and other experienced personnel. It is important to create a friendly and result-oriented work culture in the store. It may be appropriate to divide responsibilities among people clearly in terms of giving charge of category maintenance and shelf maintenance, goods receipt, door delivery, etc. in addition to selling responsibility.

Monitor Some Basic Reports for Ensuring Store Performance

Successful retailers monitor a few standard reports on a daily, weekly and monthly basis so that they can ensure the progress and growth of the store.

- *Sales achievement Percentage against Target:* A fundamental need in retailing is to know how much sales the store should achieve every day/week/month. The sales follow-up must begin with a daily target defined for the store based on the pattern of sales for every day in the week. A Saturday's target may be higher if many shoppers buy on a weekend. This can be monitored on a weekly and monthly cumulative basis also.
- *Sales Percentage against Stock:* Percentage of sales from stock must be monitored on a daily/weekly/monthly basis for every SKU for achieving the best results of proper stock holding. This measure needs to be watched closely for every category and for the whole store as well.
- *Ageing Stock Report:* Any basic merchandise management system can give out a stock-ageing report and give alerts a month in advance to help clear expiring products.
- *Top 50 SKUs:* Identify and monitor the top 50 selling SKUs in the store so that there is no out-of-stock situation relating to the fast-moving stocks in the store.
- *Bottom 50 SKUs:* Also one may need to keep a close watch on the laggards so that the store staff can promote them fast

or return a few stocks to the suppliers and refrain from buying large quantities of slow sellers.

- *Sales/Gross Margin per Store Staff:* The sales value in total divided by the number of people employed in the store can give the average sales per employee. If the same is calculated on the gross margins per employee one can arrive at the Gross Margin Return on Labour (GMROL) for the store. This will also become handy to decide the number of people to be employed in the store. If a store achieves ₹250,000 sales per month and 5 people are employed in all, then if one more person has to be employed, the sales have to be increased to ₹300,000.
- *Ratio of Total Operating Expenses to Turnover:* The total store-operating cost is the sum of all operating costs such as rental/store occupancy cost, employment cost, electricity, telephone, housekeeping, travel, sales promotion and marketing cost and other store-operations-related expenses, and it is measured as a percentage to turnover achieved in the store for a certain period like a month.

Keep the Store Clean and Neat

It is necessary for a small and medium retail store to be kept neat and clean always. Every item in the store should have its place and things have to be put back in their original places after use. For example, packaging is a big task in any small retail store and bags have to be kept ready in the place allotted to them. Many stores keep a lot of things around space often used such as the weighing area and the cash counter, and often people push things down under shelves which may even attract rodents and pests. The retailer must check the cleanliness of all the spaces in the store regularly for ensuring proper housekeeping.

Bear in mind the following points to ensure efficient store operations:

- Small and medium retail stores may open early and close late in order to ensure convenience of buying to customers. Stores ought to open on time every day. Many owners of family-run retail stores may tend to close their stores for their personal reasons, family functions, etc. Small retailers have to gain credibility of operations with customers.
- A small and medium retailer must be legally secure having done proper registration under all licences and must comply with labour regulations.
- The store stock presentation and maintenance have to be done well. It may be very easy to find the stocks on the shelves and serve customers fast.
- Training store staff on service and monitoring the performance of store staff should become a culture with the operations of the store.
- Store performance goals and targets can be defined to achieve and this will help work towards common objectives and would develop good team spirit among all store personnel.
- Faster and prompter store and door delivery services can help small and medium retailers gain a distinct competitive edge over large retailers.
- Define your own set of daily/weekly/monthly reports to follow up for performance and growth in sales.

Ensuring Operational Excellence: Viveks Limited, Chennai

The very first small store of Vivek & Company was launched on 3 May 1965 by Mr B. A. Kodandarama Setty's younger brother Mr Lakshminarayana Setty, as a 400 square feet shop on Royapettah High Road, Mylapore, Chennai (then Madras). It was a time when people's lifestyles were modest and, hence, the requirement of household products was minimal. In the small store premises, Vivek & Co. sold the typical household durables such as folding chairs, radios and bicycles, which were the common household needs for the middle-class families.

The store's winning formula, from the beginning, was to provide best quality products to customers, presented in an excellent display in the store while adopting highly ethical business practices which were not very common during those days of product shortage. Mr Kodandarama Setty constantly looked for an opportunity to expand the product range in the store while seeking newer means of reaching out to customers. He felt it was important to go for relationship building not only with customers but also with vendors and banks that he deemed as important stakeholders in business. This helped Vivek & Co. earn great goodwill from all of them. Relationships resulted in having not only timely supplies from vendors but also in gaining good margins as the scale and quantities of sales merited. Mr Kodandarama Setty says that he would personally travel to places where vendors were located to meet them and seek supplies at good prices so that they could pass on price benefits to customers.

Vivek & Co. was managed with the family's total backing. In the initial stages the family faced a setback. While the founder, Mr B. A. Lakshminarayana Setty, died within three years of launching Vivek & Co., Mr Setty's father steered the business and he provided enormous support through his rich trading experience. Retailing talents were in the family blood and the father could add significant value to the business. It was then that the family decided to shift from their native place of Kolar Gold Fields (KGF) to Chennai. The father, Mr Setty, was also a great moral support encouraging Mr Kodandarama Setty and his brothers till his last. Mr Kodandarama Setty took over when his younger brother died in 1968. He says, 'We had just one small store at that time. However, once we started building strength winning customer trust and patronage through selling quality products at fair prices and providing good service, I did start dreaming of ways and means of building the business'. The family could have basked in the success of the first store of Vivek & Co. but as a young and energetic businessman Mr Kodandarama Setty devised plans to expand the business.

Mr Kodandarama Setty opened the second store in 1968 in Purasawalkam. In 1974, he shifted the first store to more spacious premises on the same road in Luz Corner where it still operates. Mr B. A. Chandrashekara, younger brother of Mr Kodandarama Setty, took charge of the second store. The third store was opened only in 1980 when his youngest brother, Mr B. A. Srinivasa, came out of his engineering college and was able to take charge of the new store. Those days the family was particular that one of the family members should be available to run each store. Hence, they waited till 1980. The fourth and subsequent stores were opened only starting 1995. When the economy was opened up, it opened the floodgates to transnational players, and from a shortage situation, the market got access to more than adequate supplies especially of appliance brands. Mr Kodandarama Setty says, 'That was the time I could see an opportunity for us to capitalize by expansion'. Since I had large-scale expansion plans, I decided to create a limited company which would help us to meet our requirements of substantial funding from banks and financial institutions, as well as to attract professionals and experts in retailing. Internal accruals and bank funding helped us to venture out of Chennai as well and open stores in other locations such as Salem in Tamil Nadu and in Bengaluru in 1995 while increasing the number of retail outlets in Chennai itself.

To start with, way back in the 1960s, Mr Kodandarama Setty looked at developing Viveks as a multilocational retail set-up, which people now call a retail chain. One can say that Viveks was a retail chain long before retailing in India came of age in the 1990s. So, when Viveks opened a large store in Purasawalkam, people thought they were overreaching. This did not prevent the company from moving forward with plans of creating a chain of stores under the Viveks banner. Mr Kodandarama Setty avers, 'My dreams really came true only in the nineties when the economic reforms took shape. All the customer goodwill and vendor goodwill we built up came to our support when we decided to expand and created Vivek Limited in 1994. From thereon, we have been growing though our growth has not been as steady as it could have been due to various factors. We have now reached a point where we need not look back'. To increase the pace of expansion, Mr Kodandarama Setty went for a friendly takeover of Jainson, a 14-store chain which was operating across the state of Tamil Nadu, and later expanded this brand which was retained as an independent brand because of its own strength in the upcountry market in Tamil Nadu. The pace of growth shows how the company has moved from a turnover of ₹160,000 in 1965 to ₹4.67 billion in 2012_2013.

Selling home appliances was big challenge in the early days of growth of the company. It often involved selling a new concept to the consumers which is better done with live demonstration of the appliances. Mr Kodandarama Setty says, 'I adopted the demonstration route and can say with pride that Viveks was instrumental in promoting a brand like Sumeet through live demonstrations. The brand got established strongly and found customer acceptance. Not only did we conduct live demos at our stores, but also we sent our people to customers' place to give them a demo of how to use the product which helped us have a good consumer connect and improve sales as well'. The next innovative effort by Viveks Ltd was in the area of sales promotion that catapulted the company to great popularity in Chennai and in Tamil Nadu later. Mr Setty says with pride, 'I went for innovative promotions. Viveks' New Year Super Sale was launched under my leadership on 1 January 1998 with the concept of offering all our customers products at cost price for one day in the year as a thanksgiving for their year-long patronage. This was received extremely well by our customers. This led to other retailers including retailers from other verticals launching New Year Sale, which, today, has become a major annual event in Tamil Nadu. Similarly, we launched "Aadi" Sale during this Tamil month, which is considered as an inauspicious month for any purchase. People shed this belief and started buying during the month. We were also the first in launching Exhibition Sale of products and now it is a regular feature in retail particularly in Tamil Nadu'.

After sales service is key to keep the customer satisfied. One of the most important initiatives taken by the company was to establish a strong service set-up by launching Viveks Service Centre which has now grown into the largest and perhaps the only multi-product, multi-brand service centre in the country, authorized by 35 brands. Viveks Service Centre provides installation, warranty and post-warranty services to customers for a plethora of products. The service centre has a team of about 300 technicians and a strong call centre which is in constant touch with customers. The company has also recently launched its concept service wing namely Home Serve to provide homes in Chennai, not only an integrated service for all appliances alone but also to provide other key domestic services such as plumbing, electrical and carpentry. This is offered as an annual contract and the company has been constantly adding clientele for this service. In the year 2010, considering the huge market for IT products, and the importance of attracting the aspiring younger generation who look for a single stop facility for CD (Consumer Durables) and IT products, the company launched IT products in many of Viveks' counters and started selling laptops, desktops, printers, accessories etc. Viveks also felt that an independent and smaller format for IT and telecom products only could be viable if launched in a mall, which has its own heavy natural flow of traffic. This led to the opening of the company's first IT store branded as Viveks Digital 1, in 600 square feet at the Forum Mall in Koramangala, Bengaluru. The concept store has been steadily growing. In 2013, the second store in this format was launched at the Forum Vijaya Mall in Chennai, in a larger area of 1,500 square feet.

Viveks has been building the company on a strong base of two pillars, namely, customer trust and customer service, something Viveks stands for. These pillars have been the driving force to build competitive advantage including the core competency in service. The company also offers extended warranty to customers exclusively from Viveks with no dependence on their vendors. This, coupled with Viveks Service Centre, Home Serve and similar factors give adequate ammunition to combat any kind of competition, be it from domestic large business houses or international players. Viveks' consumer connect is very strong as it always worked on building customer relationship. Constantly changing customer expectations and meeting them are the basis of anything Viveks does, and customer trust and customer service are the prime foundations of Viveks. Mr Setty says, 'We got the best reflection of our service efforts from the outside world when McKinsey, the global consulting firm, in their report on Indian retail sector, prepared for CII, termed Viveks as "a brand more trusted than the brands it sells". When I consider that we are selling globally reputed brands, this reinforces our belief that we can grow in the most competitive retail environment with the standards we have set for ourselves in customer service'.

Speaking about his next generation's involvement in the business, Mr Setty says, 'I have ensured that our next generation members in the family are sent to management schools not only learn modern management theory and practice, but I have seen to it that they gain hands-on working experience in functional retailing on the floors before they are assigned responsibilities in our business. Management development continues to be a part of our philosophy. Having been one of the oldest in this business, we have passed through different business environments and have built enough expertise to run this business. This also makes the business attractive to the younger generation who are, with their education and exposure, even better equipped than us to take the company forward into its next level'.

Employees, he says are the company's greatest assets and he and his family consider them as part of their extended family. There is a strong management development approach in Viveks and many of the managers have grown from entry levels in the company to managing the operations, either at the store level or at the corporate level. Training and development of employees is one of the key activities in Viveks which ensures that they are well prepared to confront issues that arise in the environment. With employee strength of over 1,200, the company's success is a clear reflection of how they have been engaging with the employees for ensuring their growth alongside the growth of the organization itself.

Viveks is now a retail chain operating 52 stores spread across Chennai, Bengaluru and 15 other cities in Tamil Nadu. Mr Setty adopts the approach of cautious optimism as he feels that a building has to be built brick-by-brick from the floor level. In his simplistic and humble style, Mr Setty says, 'Yes, we will continue to grow but not at any frenetic pace. Yet, if opportunities come our way to expand faster through acquisition route, we will look at it seriously. For the present, we are working on adding around 10 stores each year and God willing, the pace could increase in course of time. I feel it is important to strengthen our position in existing markets, where we operate and subsequently move into a regional level'.

Key Takeaways from Viveks

- Dream of building an organization.
- Learn from the operational experience of the first store.
- Provide customers with best quality products.
- Adopt ethical business standards.
- Build good relationship with customers, vendors and banks.
- Bank funding can help business grow faster.
- During expansion, open stores in the nearby, known, markets first.
- Make the retail business attractive for the next generation kin to take over. Train them well before assigning responsibilities.
- Employees are the greatest assets of the company. Consider them as extended family members.

Ensure Financial Discipline

SECRET 7

[*The retailer's ability to manage the store finances in a disciplined manner will determine the steps of his growth.*]

It is a known fact that many small retail stores do not operate with financial discipline in India. Traditional stores may not account all the sale proceeds properly. The main advantage of registering the sales and paying proper sales tax would enable the store to achieve its growth in a straightforward and transparent manner in the long run. Many small and medium retail stores may have spent even more than the actual taxes on expenses to streamline the accounts. A proper balance sheet, if maintained, may get a good rating from the banks and availing of bank funds during expansion may be easy.

Working Capital Mismanagement

Often one sees family-run retail stores taking money out of the working capital to fund property acquisition or to meet family expenses as in the case of a wedding. Family retail businesses may fail to grow because of divisions in property among family members as they grow. Some may have taken money on higher interest from private lenders and their businesses may have seen a natural end. Many small and medium family-run stores do not expand in number because of lack of money to fund the expansion. Credit worthiness can only come from proper maintenance of accounts and administration. Further, since growth may be stifled because of lack of transparency in accounting, growth prospects become limited and the business tends to die with the generation handling it. If the small retail business grows into an organization of a chain of stores, the next generation would definitely be interested in getting into the business. Small and medium retail businesses have to ensure proper working capital management and proper accounting as well. Small storeowners too have to treat every working family individual as an employee and give each one a defined salary to manage within the means. Only then every family-run retail store can expand. We have come across instances of family retail business owners, often taking money from the sale proceeds and, eventually, we have seen the doom of their business. Successful retail stores have a history of following financial discipline and financial hygiene in their businesses.

Good Accounting Practices

Planning Operating Expenses

Store profitability is ensured only by increasing the gross margin and reducing the expenses of the store. It is very difficult in a food and grocery retail store to achieve big gross margins. Every small and medium store must be conscious about the store's gross margin. Better negotiating and buying skills can achieve greater margins. Also, one can develop the store's own repacking and branding as a private label and this can substantially increase the gross margin. There are many expenses that need to be planned in a store. Even if the store premises happen to be the family's own, notional rental value has to be considered as otherwise if given away on rent, the premises would beget the market rental value. Similarly, even for every working member salary has to be considered to be paid. Every operating expense head can be monitored on a monthly basis. If the volume of sales is increased and the expenses are reduced, gross margins will automatically increase. One cannot do anything to reduce fixed expenses such as rent and salaries, but the retailer can try and reduce other variable operating expenses. Efforts must be continuously made to increase the margins to achieve greater profitability.

	Operating Profit & Loss
	Year 1
Sales	*100*
Cost of Goods Sold (COGS)	*42.30%*
Gross Margin	19.90%
Dump	1.00%
Shrink	1.00%
Gross Margin after Dump & Shrink	17.90%
Staff Expenses	3.75%

	Operating Profit & Loss
	Year 1
Rental	3.00%
Electricity & Utilities	1.50%
Consumables	0.50%
Facility Management	0.50%
Sales Promotion & Advertisement	0.50%
Bank/Finance Charges	0.50%
License Fees	0.10%
Stationery, Conveyance & Others	1.00%
Supply Chain Cost	1.50%
Store EBITDA	**5.05%**

- Sales is the sales turnover the store makes net of taxes and discounts.
- COGS is the total cost at which a product is bought by the store.
- Gross margin is the gross profit on a product, which is the difference between the price at which it is sold and the cost at which it is bought (Selling Price − Cost = Gross Margin).
- Dump is the spoiled, perished, expired and un-saleable items thrown away from the store as waste.
- Shrink is the difference in purchased quantity and the quantity available in the store to sell. If 100 kg of rice is bought in the store to sell, the stock at the end of it all sold may only be 99.5 kg and 500 g may have been spilt off. In the case of packaged products, it is the net stocks after pilferage and shoplifting, if any, that is available to sell and, hence, the loss is known as shrink.

- Staff expenses relate to the salary and incentives paid to the staff. Often performance-linked incentives boost sales in a retail store. These are also called employment expenses as all the expenses related to staff paid by the company on staff welfare such as employee insurance, refreshment expenses and so on are included under this head.
- Rental expenses are the monthly rent payable for the store premises—either actual or notional, and it also includes property maintenance charges, property taxes, if any, paid on an annual basis also. These expenses are also called occupancy expenses because they not only include the rent but also other related expenses such as taxes and maintenance.
- Electricity expense is a variable electricity consumption bill amount paid every month for the store.
- Consumables are the packing materials, cleaning materials and other materials such as billing roll paper, and so on used in the store and the expenses incurred on those are referred to as expenses on consumables.
- Facility management expenses relate to housekeeping, security and administration and the expenses incurred usually are on cleaning the store and on security aspects.
- Sales promotion expenses relate to the money spent on advertising and sales promotions, calls made to customers, handbills distributed to customers, etc.
- Bank/finance charges are those incurred as bank commissions on fund transfers and demand drafts and interest, if any, paid on borrowings.
- License fee expenses are those paid as license renewal fees and registration expenses.
- Stationery, conveyance and others are self-explanatory. Conveyance refers to the travelling expenses that the store personnel incur on going to the wholesale markets/distributors to buy and other official travel expenses. Others may be the telephone and mailing charges, etc.

- Supply chain cost relates to the logistics and transportation expenses incurred on bringing the manufactured/purchased products to the store and the expenses incurred on door delivery of products to customers.
- Store EBITDA is the Earning Before Interest, Taxes, Depreciation and Amortization.

It is the financial discipline that safeguards a retail business, and if a retailer is careful about the expenses, he gets to earn more. The retailer's efforts should be focused on increasing the margins by all means and reducing any wastage. In the Operating Profit & Loss (P&L) table given earlier, we can see all the given expense ratios to be measured against the turnover (sales), and small and medium retailers in India have to develop the financial consciousness without leaving it only for the big businesses to follow.

Perpetual Stock-take

Proper inventory control in a retail store can be achieved not only by following the right accounting discipline but also by periodically reconciling the books of accounts with the physical inventory remaining in the store. A monthly stock-take is suggested for ensuring proper reconciliation between the stock and cash accounting of a retail store. The closing inventories of the store are physically counted in a stock-take process. Stock purchases are added SKU-wise to the opening stock and the sales are deducted from the stocks to check the veracity of the number of items in stock in the store. When multiplied by the value of each item in stock, one can get the actual value of closing stock of the store as well. Stock-take must be done both by quantity of each SKU and by its MRP value. For all the quantities of stock the MRP value also could be assigned and one can check the opening stock value, value of the purchased stock, value of the sold stock and the value of the closing stock. This process is known as a perpetual stock-take as stock reconciliation is repeated every month, usually on the last day of the month after working hours. The major advantage of such perpetual stock-take is the determination of the veracity of sales and stock figures including the quantity and value of the missing and un-saleable stock—that is, the 'shrinkage' in a retail store.

Plough Back at Least 30 Per Cent of Profits into the Business

The best financial practice to keep the store growing is to plough back at least 30 per cent of profits into the business for its future expansion. Many people who run a small or medium store do not follow the practice of ploughing back even a small part of the profit earned into the business, for its expansion and growth. This is the main reason why the small retail business struggles to grow. If a retailer is willing to put a good part of the profits back into the business, he will get enough money to expand his store and open more stores as well. Reinvesting part of the profits into the business is the first step towards funding a retail store's expansion. The second step may involve raising funds by short-term overdrafts and loans from the bank and the third step may be to look up to investors of various genres including the phased dilution of equity both to achieve growth and create wealth. It is essential for a small retailer to initially fund the business carefully to achieve growth.

In the current scenario, for the small and medium retail business to achieve significant growth with all its numerous SKUs and wide customer base to serve, following the financial hygiene to account for every paisa while prudently funding the business is of paramount importance.

Hard Work and Zero Debt: Sethwala Foods Limited, Mumbai

Mr Mudar Sethwala is an epitome of hard work. With a humble educational qualification of Standard 8, he started working in retail sales and service in Mumbai's first department store called Akbarally's in Chembur in 1980. Driven by the dire need to earn as he hailed from an economically backward family background, he would often buy different kinds of products sold at less prices and discounts in the market and sell them to various retailers as a part-time business, on holidays and off-shift hours. Mudar says that he learnt the art of selling and interacting with customers at Akbarally's. He left the department store after a year and began to sell perfumes to retail shops in Mumbai. As he visited many retail stores, he came to understand the demand for various other products and began to trade in multifarious goods by buying at lesser prices from wholesale markets and selling them to small retailers at a profit.

Spotting his selling capabilities, his uncle (mother's brother) who was running a franchise outlet for the Mongini's brand of cake shop in Borivali in Mumbai invited him to join his store to help him in the business as his parents did not like him doing the tedious local travelling every day that was involved in the trading. His uncle paid him a monthly salary of ₹325. The yearning to earn surfaced in him again. Not being satisfied with the salary within three months of joining, when the Mongini's shop was averaging a sales figure of ₹20,000 per month, he asked his uncle what sales target he would expect him to achieve. His uncle told him that he would like a monthly average sale of ₹35,000 and if the figure was achieved he would be paid a monthly salary of ₹750 per month. He not only achieved the average sales target of ₹35,000 per month, but surpassed it as well within the next three months. He says, 'I spoke to every customer and recommended higher value cakes and delicacies. I also suggested more items to each customer. Soon, I came to know many of my regular customers personally and that was the secret of my success'. Then his uncle gave him full charge of the shop. He struck a fresh deal with his uncle saying that he'll open the shop on the weekly holiday of Thursday and that the profit they make on that day would be shared equally on a 50:50 basis. The amount of sales he made on the four holidays in the month and the profit he made in the shop was more than his monthly salary and his uncle was impressed with him a great deal. From the time he started making such good profits, his salary went up within a year to ₹2,000 per month. He was really encouraged when his uncle gave him charge of the shop for a fixed amount of profit to be given to him every month and the balance could be enjoyed by him. He took the sales up to ₹300,000 per month. So Mudar with his selling abilities could catapult the average monthly sales within three years from a meagre ₹20,000 per month to ₹300,000 per month. He says,

> The location of the shop was a busy one being near the Borivili railway station and I had to see that every customer is served with speed while I do suggestive selling as well. Further, as people in Mumbai would go early to catch trains for work and would return late as well, I spotted an opportunity to open the store early, sometimes as early as 7 o'clock and close by late night. This resulted in gaining many customers for my shop.

His brother Mr Saifee Sethwala in his free time during schooling would often help him in the shop when Mudar had his breaks. As his uncle wanted the store back, at the end of three years he handed over the Mongini's shop back to him for his sons to manage.

By then Mudar had become a popular shopkeeper in the Borivili railway station area. With the money he earned by innovatively working in his uncle's Mongini's shop, he opened a *kirana* shop just next to his uncle's shop in 1984. He told both Mr Zoher Korakiwala, the Chairman of Mongini's brand of cake shops, and his uncle that he would not open any competing cake shop or bakery or for that matter he would not sell from his new *kirana* shop any item that was sold from the Mongini's shop. Mudar named his *kirana* shop, 'Centre Point'. He says,

> I focused all my attention towards serving my customers with their daily ration needs from Centre Point, a store spread over just 200 square feet. The uniqueness of the store was the merchandise mix that I planned for the store. I sold chicken and meat products from a cold storage facility within the store in addition to grocery. That made the difference for more people to come to my store. Moreover I sold at very competitive prices and gained customer trust.

In the meantime, in 1985, as his uncle's Mongini's cake shop was up for sale, Mudar with the help of two other partners purchased the store along with its franchise rights and the same shop crossed a turnover of ₹700,000 a month within a decade and, eventually, exceeded a turnover of ₹10 million per annum. Mudar expanded his cake shop operations further opening new Mongini's stores under partnerships in Kandivali and Vasai in Mumbai suburbs, which are even today doing sound retail business. His younger brother Mr Salim Sethwala started helping him in Centre Point operations and in chicken purchase and sales. As Salim joined the business soon after completing his graduation, the family opened multiple Centre Point stores in a chain format and they now operate around 15 stores, each in an area ranging from 200_250 square feet selling chicken products and grocery items. Centre Point *kirana* stores operate all over the suburbs and outskirts of Mumbai such as Thane, Biwandi, Dahisar, Mira Road, I. C. Colony, Borivali, Kandivali, Vasai and Lonavla. Mudra says,

> The store is well organized and every Centre point outlet is an efficiently operating one with positive bottom-lines. The focus is on

reducing operating costs and increasing margins at every available opportunity. As a significant part of the turnover in each Centre Point comes from our backward integrated chicken and chicken products which form part of the merchandise plan for the store, we make good profits that make faster expansion possible.

Mudar and his brothers now plan to open more Centre Point stores across the city of Mumbai.

Subsequently, the youngest brother Mr Quraish Sethwala too joined in and Mudar and his brothers opened exclusive semi-wholesale and retail shops to sell chicken and chicken products in the Municipal Market, Borivili, which cater to the needs of local hoteliers and restaurateurs. The business of trading and wholesaling and retailing chicken and ready-to-eat chicken products grew, as the family became distributors for various chicken processors and suppliers since the early 2000s. As processed chicken gained a good deal of market share, Mudar and his brothers established a chicken processing unit initially as a semi-automatic line and later as a fully automatic state-of-the-art processing unit by Stork from Holland, in Talasari, Maharashtra. It now has a capacity to process around 20 tonnes in a single shift. The unit supplies chicken to a number of institutions including large hotels on an annual contract basis.

Mudar's parents were a great support to the brothers in their business. His father expired in 1997 and his mother continues to inspire them. Mudar says that she is the heart of their family and she advises him to maintain relationships to mutually grow in the business. Speaking about the family's involvement in the retail business, Mudar says,

> The support of the entire family is critical for the success of the retail business. My wife Tasneem, Salim's wife Farida, Saifee's wife Alifya and Quraish's wife Yasmin are all educationally more qualified than all of us brothers and they render a helping hand from behind the

scene, often bringing relevant solutions to the many business problems we discuss'. The family yet closely holds the retail business, which has crossed a turnover of ₹440 million in the financial year 2015_2016. Quite a surprising aspect of Mr Mudar Sethwala's business is its current zero debt financial discipline. A company run true to a strict financial discipline, it depends only on internal accruals.

Mudar's ability to spot opportunities and to hit upon the right product offerings in the right time has put him at a clear advantage to gain growth in his retail business. He identified the right locations at the right cost so that he could ensure a robust bottom-line, which eventually helped him grow faster. He plans for a big rollout of both his *kirana* retail chain business, Centre Point, and for expanding his chicken business as well.

Key Takeaways from Sethwala Foods

- Spot opportunities in the right markets and in the right locations.
- Follow the 'Golden Word' formula and always suggest to customers more products and upsell at every opportunity.
- Keep the format in the right size to keep expenses low as internal accruals only would matter more for funding expansion initially.
- Understand specific customer needs and open niche product-lines to offer customers.
- Constantly look for growth opportunities.
- Improve business and grow steadily.
- Plan to open more stores as you turn the very first store profitable.
- Follow a strict financial discipline.

Adopt Simple Store Systems

SECRET 8

[
In the current scenario of even a small store carrying a large number of SKUs, it is worthwhile to deploy affordable IT applications like the simple POS system to understand the details of what have been sold and what have to be stocked.
]

Information is always a source of strength for any retailer. In earlier days, when the store sizes were small, the store had very fewer products, and information on sales and stock could be on anyone's fingertips. Now that the product range is big and the number of customers who come to the store also has increased, information needs to be gathered properly. Manual means of gathering such information may be very difficult now.

Information in retailing is the key to achieve growth in all functions. It is relevant to keep a record of all the purchases and sales in the store so that the retailer can understand and know the exact progress of the business from time to time. Many retailers may think that computerization of the business is cumbersome and difficult to maintain. Many others may think that it is hard to find the right people to operate the system and it may be expensive too. Systems are so simple with applications similar to those on the mobile phone and so they can be easily handled with training. Further, systems like the CCTV security system can be integrated with smart phones and the retailer can see his store from wherever he is.

POS: The POS is a billing system. It does not require huge investments as was the case in the past. All that one needs is a computer system in the store. Now we have POS and other retail-related softwares available on the cloud platform. That means the software is available for a monthly payment of amounts ranging from ₹700 per month to ₹1,500 per month, depending upon the functional systems and the number of reports required. Many retail POS and Merchandise Management System (MMS) solutions organizations offer the software support hosting the whole system on their own servers in order to reduce expenses and investments for small and medium retailers. POS can also be integrated with smart phones and the retailer can see at any point in time from anywhere how much billing has been made in the store during his absence.

Efficient IT systems will enable the store to prevent fraud. POS system leaves a trail of all the activities on the POS and each bill can be systematically followed by the serial number. The bills made are systematically recorded in the system and bill cancellation or item cancellation can be clearly tracked. Staff can be given user codes and the retailer can find out who has made a bill or used the system at any point in time. Item cancellation and bill cancellation rights can be held with the storeowner or manager, to prevent fraud.

MMS: MMS helps in end-to-end inventory management in a retail store. It handles and supports the functions of planning the base stock of the store, stock ordering, receiving, transferring for stock returns and inter-transfer between branches if any. The MMS system controls information on inventories by receiving data from POS and adjusts stocks accordingly. The retailer has to only check the physical closing stocks to see whether the stocks tally with the stocks shown by MMS. So, the MMS can perform the major merchandise functions of sale recording, stock ordering and procurement, storage and distribution. It can also generate reports relating to merchandise management. The system can give the closing stock of any item/product at any point in time; it can be programmed to give information on the top selling SKU, top-margin-yielding SKUs and on the ageing of stocks as well. The dashboard of information and reports can be set with the aforementioned reports for the storeowner/manager to see at anytime, which may be very convenient for leading the store towards growth.

Financial System

Both the POS and MMS can integrate with any financial and accounting system. When the store's POS and MMS operate on the cloud, the day's sales details as end-of-day reconciliation can be integrated into the accounting system seamlessly. Taxation and other reports too can be generated easily. At any point in time the storeowner or manager can know the store's P&L easily. Also in a computerized financial system, monthly stock-takes could be automatically done with ease.

As costs have come down drastically on cloud-based systems and their operations, IT systems can be used in small- and medium-sized retail stores. These systems are easy-to-use at an operating level with limited training involved. Many small stores in cities have already begun to avail the services of retail IT hosting companies at lower expenses. The adoption of IT in small pharmaceutical stores and small and medium organized sweet stores has been pretty fast. It is only a matter of time before small and medium grocery stores adopt IT systems in their stores, which will automatically bring in the best practices of small store retailing.

The following are some of the key stocks and sales reports generated by the system on demand:

- Daily Sales Report
- Weekly/Monthly Sales Summary
  - By Category
  - By SKU

- Daily Stock Report
  - By Category
  - By SKU
- Percentage of Sale from Stock Report
  - By Category up to SKU Level
- Inventory Valuation Report
- Cost of Goods Sold Report
- Stock Purchase Report
- Store P&L and Balance Sheet

Above all, fast service supported by an able IT system enables splendid customer experience. Faster service provided by the retailer will always result in customer satisfaction. IT systems can ensure efficient stock management and, hence, the required stocks may be always available in the store. The system also helps the store to have the SKUs in a controlled manner and not let choices of products go unwieldy and wide. The merchandise hierarchy concept enabled by the system will clearly help the store staff understand the rate of sale and stock levels starting from a higher category level to the lowest SKU level.

Rewrite Rules; Retain Values: Future Group, Mumbai

The erstwhile Pantaloons, once owned by Kishore Biyani (referred fondly as KB) has a great story to tell. It originated from a meagre effort by KB who hailed from a humble merchant family background, to sell trouser lengths to people working in the Mumbai offices. He thought differently and engaged college students who worked in their spare time (colleges worked in shifts in Mumbai, that left students with a good deal of spare time!) to sell trouser pieces and collected proceeds in easy instalments, otherwise known nowadays as equated monthly instalments. He created unique part-time employment way back in the early 1980s for the youth in Mumbai. From such humble beginning to becoming a big corporate conglomerate is not an easy task. Retailing was second skin to KB as he took to meeting customers strategically in a direct-to-home effort. He then opened his first small retail store near the Andheri railway station, in a two-tiered floor format. It had the brand name Pantaloons (meaning a man's close fitting garment from the waist and the legs), written as a brand logo in its own unique style. Quite early enough, he adopted good processes including the creation of a back-end manufacturing and sourcing infrastructure, integrated by technology systems.

The story goes that Shoppers Stop refused to keep KB's brands as shop-in-shop in their outlets. Outraged by the refusal, KB focused on his own retailing efforts and opened his first large department store in Kolkata in 1997. The only competition coming up that time was Shoppers Stop in the department store category. Cautious expansion was the growth mantra of Shoppers Stop. Crossroads, the first mall in Haji Ali, Mumbai, supported KB as did the Phoenix Mills mall in Lower Parel, Mumbai by giving space on lease in 1999 and since then Pantaloons rolled out their department stores with their own private labels in a big way in India. The company was the first in the retail sector to embrace an enterprise resource planning (ERP) system called BAAN, for ensuring process-oriented business operations (later as the business grew, the company implemented SAP).

The big expansion spree was hit upon in 1999 with the success of the establishment of Big Bazaar as a hypermarket with grocery and staples as core categories of merchandise. The merchandise mix was a fusion of grocery and apparel and the first store in Bengaluru was promoted as a common man's store with down-to-earth pricing. The business strategy was such that one could bring anything for exchange and a certain value per kilogram was given for redemption on the next purchase. Many Big Bazaars opened and the company Pantaloon Retail India Limited (PRIL) was a big success. As it was already a listed company, many eyes were on PRIL and its performance. KB did a good job and expanded the Big Bazaar stores to a number more than 100 soon.

Strategic sales promotions were key to the success of the business at Big Bazaar. The National Holiday Sales strategies saw near-stampede in stores and it would be no exaggeration if we said that these promotions were a big runway success. The 26 January sales or the 15 August sales did go down well with bargain-seeking customers and they thronged the store. As the available space in the stores could not often contain the humongous footfalls, store vigilance became a great concern.

KB began investing in many brands as a strategy to make money and it paid as an investment strategy. KB was the architect of many innovations in retailing and one among them was the seamless mall that he discovered known as Central. He spotted opportunities to co-invest with brands as a strategy for the group as policies of FDI in single-brand retailing changed in the country to favour investments in India. KB was the one who took maximum advantage of brands that took the initiative to grow by co-investing and reaping the returns.

The group ran into a cash crunch a few years ago, mainly as a result of its diversification into non-allied businesses. The company was forced to sell the Pantaloons department store chain to Aditya Birla Retail to wriggle itself out of its debts. KB instantly divested his stakes in non-core businesses considerably and began to focus on his core retail business. Competition in the sector grew with big entrants opening many retail formats at a breakneck speed. For the first time, a few years ago the sales figures of Reliance Retail pipped Future Group at the post, to emerge a leader in revenues pushing KB's retail business to the no. 2 slot in India. But KB was not deterred as he had his plans up his sleeves.

KB did bounce back soon. After this brief period of turmoil, KB managed to run his Big Bazaar stores and other retail formats under Future Retail Ltd in his own inimitable full throttled ease. While his Big Bazaar grew to become 300 stores in 100 cities, he not only gathered the financial gall to acquire retail entities such as Heritage (Hyderabad), Nilgris (Bengaluru), Easyday (acquired from Bharti Retail, New Delhi) and Hypercity (Mumbai) but also innovated the new concepts of KB Retail Shops, gourmet retail by name Food Hall, etc. besides creating a plethora of private label products as FMCG with his own exclusive manufacturing facilities. The Future Group has undoubtedly emerged as the country's leader in the modern supermarket and hypermarket categories. Kishore Biyani, with his exemplary retailing talents and determination is an example of how a man from a humble middle class background could excel, spotting opportunities in the growing retail market in India.

Key Takeaways from Future Retail

- Think big. You can become no. 1.
- Spot opportunities and act immediately.
- When any door is seen closed, make another way to grow.
- Do not be afraid of setbacks. Work out your plan to excel.
- Speed of growth is the essence of success.
- Create your own back-end support to cater to your needs.
- Expand into a variety of formats to lead the pack and succeed.

Promote the Store

SECRET 9

[*In a world of intense competition, a retailer has to be constantly in touch with customers, not only to remain in their minds but hearts too!*]

The small and medium retail segment in India seldom makes any marketing and communication effort to get customers to come to the store and buy. This is because the retailers are usually contented with the number of people who come to the store regularly. In a situation where the local competition is high, it may make a lot more sense to market the store to the customers.

Above-the-line Marketing

Any advertisement in the media such as the print media, television and radio is referred to as above-the-line communication. Cost-effective communication is necessary for marketing the retail store. Such above-the-line media are used when a retail store wishes to get customers to come to the store in an effort to create footfalls.

Handbills (fliers) and Newspaper Inserts: Because the print media in India is very expensive and it may cause a good deal of spill—going over and above the spread of target segment of customers—newspaper advertising is avoided by MSME. Instead, it is advisable to advertise through printed handbills to be distributed to customers and the same can be used as inserts in newspapers in the targeted localities. Handbill distribution is inexpensive and it can have the desired reach as well without any spill. The handbill can carry messages of the offers and promotions of products and services. As many housing societies and flat associations are there in colonies even in small towns, the handbills can be an effective medium of communication. During times of new product introduction or during the introduction of new schemes, handbills are said to be effective.

Radio: FM Radio is quite popular in all the towns of India now. The reach of FM radio is good, but it is yet an unaffordable medium for MSME as even non-prime time spots are very expensive. Jingles and radio spots usually in the form of announcements of schemes and promotions could be done if customers have to be invited to the store to avail them. Cost-effective communication by radio is usually in the form of announcements because recording a jingle or creating a radio spot in the form of an enacted conversation and broadcasting it may be more expensive. Since the reach of the FM radio is across the whole town, it may cover a much larger area than the catchment of the retail store and, hence, there could be a good amount of advertisement spill and wastage.

TV: Television advertisements are usually done by MSME using the local cable TV channel. These advertisement and communication messages are usually in the form of message crawlers. Simple announcements, greetings and festival wishes could be conveyed by stores via the cable TV local channel to the customers.

Below-the-line Marketing

The marketing activities and communication efforts made in the store premises are classified under below-the-line marketing efforts.

There are a few marketing activities listed below that are usually done by MSME.

Displays, Visual Merchandising and Display Contests: Displays of products with messages accompanying the displays are done on a large scale to attract the attention of customers. When products are organized in a visually appealing manner in a display with accompanying messages and props, it is known as visual merchandising. Retailers often participate in display contests. They may create display corners during the time of the contest for a brand. But one has to see that the retailer gets some additional benefits of assured returns or schemes as products are being bought for such contests. This would ensure the earning of the right additional margins for the efforts taken by the retailer to display in the contest apart from having the prospect of winning some sweepstakes if the retailer emerges as a winner or gets to have a position among the top few winners in the locality or region.

Shelf-talkers: Small and medium retailers display products on shelves or show windows using shelf-talkers for communicating with the customers. These shelf-talkers are usually in the form of starbursts and stickers that announce schemes, offers and promotions specific to a brand or a product. The shelf-talkers are pasted on the frames of the display shelves that would carry the promoted product with the sole objective of attracting customers' attention to the product and, consequently, achieve increase in the sales of the product. The shelf-talkers may be designed by the store in forms that could eventually become a signature entity for the store. The retailer could change shelf-talkers in the store anytime as they are used conveniently to promote products with discounts, consumer offers, etc.

Efficient Utilization of Shelf Space

Festoons and Bunting: Brand suppliers and distributors use the retailers' premises to hang festoons and bunting carrying advertisement of products with offers and schemes in vogue. These festoons may at times adorn the stores colourfully but the retailer has to see that the festoons and bunting are used appropriately in designated locations as eye-catchers because otherwise they may interfere with the visibility of displayed products. Festoons and bunting are used usually during festival occasions when the products are promoted aggressively and when attractive offers are given by brands and suppliers.

Hang Bunting and Danglers at Higher Levels for an Unobstructed View of the Store

Promotion by Personal Selling

In retailing, personal selling plays a major role in increasing the business. Traditional retailers have good contacts with customers, and they do not fail to acknowledge the presence of customers in the store premises. They should not fail to greet customers, ask them what they want, subtly suggest additional goods and items to buy and ask customers to buy the stocks with offers and promotions. While modern retailers may follow a structured system with a few steps of selling, traditional small- and medium-sized retailers would follow the process of personal selling subconsciously. Traditional retailers respect customers from their heart. Let's see the difference between how modern retailers serve customers and how small retailers treat them. Modern retailers follow certain steps of selling right from the time customers enter the store until they leave the store premises. Both traditional and small retailers serve customers but with differently.

	Modern	Traditional
Customer Attendance	Customer enters store, walks around, browses and picks up products.	Customer stands at the store counter and waits to be served.
Greeting	Greets customer by wishing good morning/evening, etc.	Acknowledge the very presence of customer by an instant smile and a word of welcome. Recognize customer by name. Enquire about the family too.

	Modern	Traditional
Ascertaining Needs	Salespeople may ask, 'How may I help you, please?'	Asks frankly what customer needs. Often seek the list of items or indent so that the retailer can quickly organize the items for delivery.
Handling Queries/ Objections	Responds if customer asks for any clarifications on prices, etc. as the store follows the self-service format.	Voluntarily mentions/ clarifies prices, schemes/offers and asks if customer wants more.
Sales Conclusion	Sometimes shows newly arrived items or asks customer if he/she wants any items from the impulse displays made near cash counter.	Packs and picks items fast and delivers to customer.
Payment	Often customer waits at the queue in the cash till. Cashier makes bill, swipes credit card or collects cash and bids good bye to the customer after handing over the bag.	Collects cash. Invites customer to come again.
Follow-up & Customer Service Guarantee	Follow-up is done via the customer relationship programme by emails and mobile alerts by large retailers. Product complaints/replacements are done according to store policy.	Phones up customers to ask if they would want any more stocks. Product complaints and replacements are done instantaneously by the retailer.

Mobility and Online (Digital and Social Media) Marketing

Tele-calling: The most effective way to communicate product offers and promotions is through phone calls. It is necessary for a retail store management to have a good database of its customers with all the contact details and coordinates. Calls may be made to customers to invite them to come to the store. Calls can be made to customers who have not visited the store for more than a month or for more than a certain period of time.

Short Messaging Service (SMS): In addition to tele-calls, mobile alerts and SMS could be used to communicate with customers. While modern retailers use this medium, traditional retailers may not use mobile phones smartly. This is because traditional retailers may not have the contact details of their regular customers. Similarly, digital marketing is also used in a big way nowadays by large retailers. There is every opportunity for the traditional retailers to connect with the youthful customer segments online. What is significant for traditional retailers is to have an organized recorded database with the relevant details to connect with customers without depending any longer on the customer data from memory.

Use of free SMS websites, WhatsApp and GPRS: Some websites in India enable people to send free SMS and small retailers could use the services of these websites to send SMS to customers free or on subsidized rates. WhatsApp is a big communication enabler currently, and retailers may use this application to communicate with customers. As many customers use smart phones in India, it may be worthwhile to use General Packet Radio Service (GPRS) and WhatsApp applications to alert or remind customers to buy from the store. The most attractive prices of the day could be disseminated to customer's phones using the GPRS application. Those customers walking in the vicinity of the store can also download the application and get the day's prices or any relevant product information disseminated by the store. Going forward, the GPRS facility may be very useful for MSME to disseminate information to loyal customers.

Word-of-mouth Promotions

If product promotions and service levels are high in any store, they are carried by word-of-mouth from one customer to another. Customers do speak about good service rendered by the store personnel. Service actions such as the timely replacement of a returned product or the timely door-delivery service rendered by the store are often spoken about from customer to customer. Spreading information from person to person either by word-of-mouth or by any social media is usually referred to as 'viral marketing'. Small retailers usually implore their customers to tell other customers about their products and services.

Methods of Ensuring Customer Relationship

Customer relationship pertains to creating a sticky relationship with maximum number of customers who would repeatedly visit the store. The small retailers could forge such relationship by adopting simple customer relationship practices.

Extending Credit: Small retailers in residential colonies would know every customer and often customers could call for products from the store to be delivered at their doors. These customers may be salaried families who would get their pay only once a month. The retailer could maintain a record of frequent purchases made and could collect the payment only once a month, extending credit. This is a usual practice followed by small- and medium-sized grocery and *kirana* retailers. Large retailers do not extend such credit and this becomes a clear competitive edge for the MSME segment.

Picking up Monthly Purchase Ration List for Supply: The retailer could proactively call and visit households to collect the list of monthly requirements on a fixed day during the beginning of every month and supply the same. This step may initiate the practice of stock-up buying from small retailers. Such an effort to collect the monthly grocery list will also help customers to be thoroughly loyal to the store, save other things such as the quality of products, prices and service levels are exemplary too.

Loyalty Rewards: The MSME segment retailers could think about various ways of ensuring the loyalty of customers. Loyalty rewards could be in the form of a financial reward. For instance, the store could offer an additional percentage of discount on the monthly purchases if the purchase value is above a set threshold. Or for its loyal customers, the store could offer half a kilogram of sugar or any staple household item of need free. Loyalty rewards need not necessarily be financial always. In cities, some stores run errands free of cost for their loyal customers—these errands include services such as payment of telephone bills and mobile recharge on customer's behalf using the store staff. These free services extended could be helpful for those working and old-aged loyal customers.

The success of a store's marketing efforts would largely depend upon the genuineness of efforts taken to offer the right promotions and offers and communicate them well to customers. Cost effectiveness is the prime aspect that has to be taken into consideration while planning the marketing and communication efforts for a retail store. The impact of a marketing campaign or a promotion could be measured by determining the increase in footfalls and the resultant increase in sales. Costs could be controlled if small- and medium-sized retailers could forge alliances with suppliers to co-promote products to customers and share the marketing expenses.

Baking Tasty Recipes for Her Consumers: The Sugarr & Spice, Kolkata

Married at the age of 13, in 1963, to the son of the zamindar of Murshidabad, Supriya Roy was worried about her life at a time when the zamindari system ended and along with that the family's financial condition too began to dwindle. Supriya's husband, Prosanta Kumar Roy, too was very young and was doing his master's degree when Supriya, studying in class 10, became the mother of a baby boy. She had her household challenges to face as they were not doing well financially. Supriya was always good at baking, even from childhood. She learnt how to bake well and she did it very passionately.

As the family was living in a palatial house, there was enough room for her to start baking classes. On the one hand, she began teaching baking as a passionate hobby and on the other hand, she thought that it might bring some revenues to support the family. With just one student, she started her baking and cooking classes in 1985. Soon the demand for her classes gained momentum and by word-of-mouth her baking classes became popular in the vicinity of her home in Kolkata. Supriya Roy expanded her school with appointed teachers for other crafts too such as tailoring and type-writing. She continued to run baking and cooking classes successfully while attending to the key responsibilities of taking care of her family and, especially, her growing son. When her son grew up and when she was around 40 years of age, in 1990, she was determined to chart a new course in her business by opening a small bakery to sell her tasty cakes and confectionery. She opened her bakery with her savings of about ₹300,000 in a small area of 200 square feet and named it 'The Sugarr & Spice'. Initially, she faced some resistance from her family but her husband supported her in every way. The first bakery was opened within the premises of her home which was in the vicinity of SSKM hospital in Bhowanipore. The stream of visitors to the hospital also enabled an enviable quantum of footfalls into the bakery.

The business did well as it sold the tasty creations from the expertise of Supriya Roy. Slowly, the bakery business had 12 employees and it started growing steadily. Supriya expanded the menu of products offered in the store to include more goodies for customers. Both Prosanta Kumar Roy and Supriya Roy put their efforts together and the business began to beget profits. Within five years, as the business became a solid one with robust processes both in the front-end and back-end, Supriya Roy thought that it was time she expanded the business by the franchise route. There were so many customers coming from far and near as the bakery became a destination business. People planned to visit the bakery just to go over there to buy. The business was so customer focussed that Supriya Roy knew that she could make a big success if the business was set up in many locations in the city. Supriya had enough space within her sprawling and palatial house premises to accommodate her expanding manufacturing facility in an area of 30,000 square feet. She was keen on maximizing her profits and decided to build the required business and IT systems to support a planned franchisee network.

The establishment of the franchisee network began in 1998 and within a span of 12 years, the company grew to have 100 bakery outlets spread not only in Kolkata but also in West Bengal, Odisha, Jharkhand, Bhutan and Bangladesh. The franchise route taken by the company was the right one. It was backed by a constant supply of quality products from the centralized facility, proper branding guidelines and the right operating systems and procedures. The company was registered in 1998 as a private limited one that gave enough leverage to access more secured funds for the business.

Though the business was steadily growing, it faced a setback in 2006 because a trusted employee and aide in charge of finance and accounts cheated the Roys. They weathered the tough phase and once again emerged to get back on the growth path of the business. Supriya Roy began to personally supervise finances of the organization taking the setback as a lesson well learned not to repeat any such carelessness in future.

The result of her hard work has earned her as many as 125 stores and more currently with over 51 products in the categories of cakes and pastries, sandwiches and burgers, pizzas and hot dogs, patties and rolls, kebabs and tandoori items, etc., in addition to chocolates, cookies and wafers in the bakery satisfying multitudes of taste buds. The trick of her trade is in the taste that Supriya has created in her offerings. She understands her customer needs, tastes and preferences thoroughly and caters to them carefully. She has now bought land in Howrah and Jalpaiguri to build more manufacturing units to support her business. Supriya Roy is keen to learn yet. She does not fail to attend the fairs and exhibitions that happen in the baking and food sector. She still works hard every day, personally supervising the business. Though her son Pallab Roy runs his own wholesale pharmacy business, her grandson helps her in the Sugarr & Spice chain of retail bakeries.

The Ministry of Small Scale Industries recognized Supriya Roy with the National Award for the Best Woman Entrepreneur in the year 2000. In 2009, her company was certified with ISO 9001:2008 standards in recognition of its robust systems and processes, the first of the kind in the bakers and confectioners category in India. In 2010, the Sugarr & Spice was awarded the MSME National Award in recognition of manufacturing outstanding quality products. Her successful efforts have resulted in setting up state-of-the-art manufacturing and retailing facilities.

With her iron will to succeed further, Supriya Roy is growing from strength to strength in the retail bakery chain category attempting to spread all over India soon.

Key Takeaways from the Sugarr & Spice

- Try what you are good at and you will succeed.
- Use already available resources for your retail business first.
- When you are not able to serve your customers from afar, go and set up stores where they are.
- Building organized systems and processes in your business can scale up your business fast.
- Expand your business by profitable means like franchising once you create your systems well.
- Expand your retail efforts within the vicinity first, before going wider.
- If you enjoy what you do, you will excel in it.

Place the Right People in the Store

SECRET 10

> *People are the assets of a retail organization. They are considered 'human capital'. The returns that they can give by delivering their responsibility towards the customers are immeasurable. The intangible assets that people can create for a retail organization by extending sheer personal service can build a big store brand eventually.*

Retailing is a people-intensive business. The retailer has to plan for placing people in his store. People are considered human capital for the retail business. Retailing has multifarious functions that are unique to the business—retail selling and customer service, ash handling, merchandise planning and buying, managing distribution and supply chain, cleaning and maintaining the store, marketing and promoting the store, etc. All these functions have to be performed by people. For new stores often one person may perform many roles. The retailer needs to decide how tasks have to be grouped to provide the highest level of efficiency. For example, in a store where customer walk-ins are less and the merchandise stocked are high fashion garments, the same salesperson may perform the task of selling, assist the customer in selection, do the billing for the customer, collect payment and pack the item too. However, in a supermarket where a cash-and-carry system exists, the job may be separate, with different people stacking items on shelves, cashiering, etc. In a store selling specialty products, like branded FMCG, there is no product development effort required from the retailer since the brands are presenting developed and advertised lines. Hence, the salesperson may only play the role of indenting for re-orders as well as selling, since he/she would know which items get sold slowly or which items are sold quickly. However, say, in a fashion garments store which has its own label, a specialist merchandiser may be required to take decisions on re-orders, to decide whether continuing the product line would benefit the store or not.

The Two Typical Roles in Retailing

Key Role 1: Selling and Extending Customer Service

Selling and customer service are the basic roles of the salesperson in the retail store. The salesperson in a retail store can increase sales if he/she is trained well. In many small retail stores, where the owner performs the role of the salesperson one can see that he/she would spare no efforts to maximize the purchases of customers and serve them with great speed. They would speak to customers to recommend products and see that maximum bill value is achieved. The person who performs the role of serving customers and selling merchandise concentrates only on customers and keeps expecting customers to visit the retail store. The moment a walk-in happens, the salesperson would first extend his/her greetings with a welcoming smile. The next quick step in the retail selling process is to enquire the specific needs of the customer. If the customer needs vermicelli and sugar, the salesperson should subtly understand that the customer is going to make 'payasam' and then recommend or remind the customer to buy other needed ingredients such as 'elaichi', cashews and 'kismis'. This would amount to cross-selling; if the customer has asked for a pack of 250 g vermicelli and if the salesperson recommends and sells a 500 g pack, the effort taken to sell a bigger pack is known as upselling. In small retail stores, personal selling assumes a good deal of significance as it can increase the sales. The customer may have some questions on quantity or shelf life or on quality which the salesperson answers using his knowledge. When the salesperson and the customer are done with the whole list of items bought, he/she prepares the cash memo and receives the cash. In the final step of the retail selling process, the salesperson hands the bags over to the customer and says, 'Thank you. Please visit again, sir/madam', with a smile always on the face.

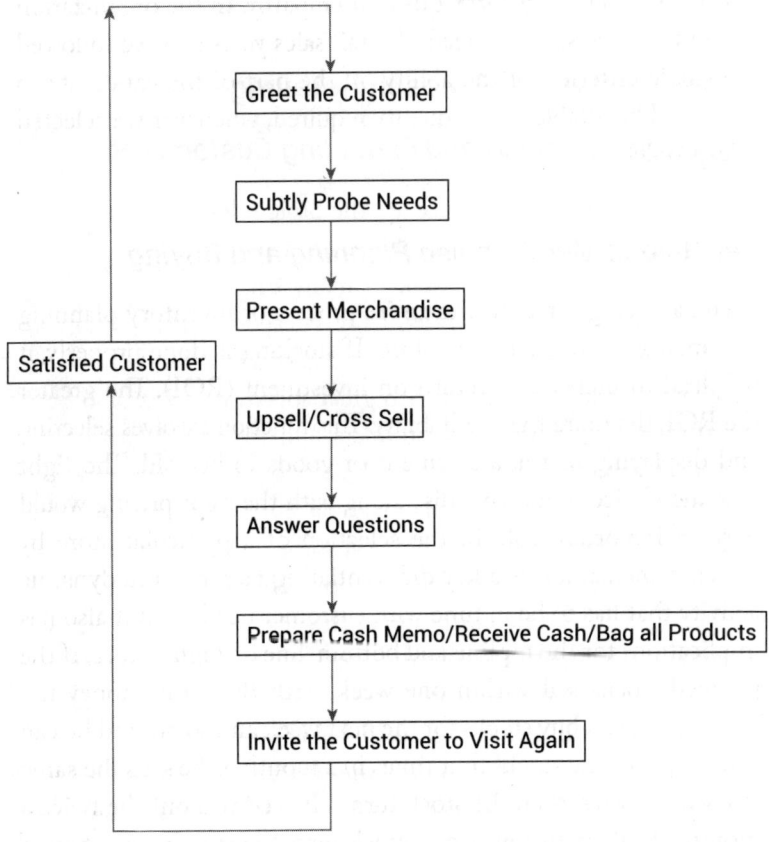

Thus, the salesperson performs a multifaceted role in a small- and medium-sized retail store. In a supermarket, as merchandise sell-through may be very fast, the salesperson may have no time to do any act of selling and serving customers. In an apparel store, following such selling process may yield good results. However, the salespersons need to be trained well to sell and serve customers always in a pleasant manner. Often the salesperson may need to perform the role of a runner and execute door deliveries as when orders for deliveries may come from customers. Retail employees performing any function have to be customer friendly and they ought to think always from the perspective of customers, exercising a great deal of empathy. In the organization where I used to serve as head of retail sales years ago, we followed the single criterion of the ability on the part of the candidate to smile and be affable as the quality required, whenever we selected salespeople.

Key Role 2: Merchandise Planning and Buying

Merchandising refers to the entire process of inventory planning and management in a retail store. If stocking is done properly, it will lead to increase in return on investment (ROI). The greater the ROI, the more the profitability. This function involves selecting and displaying of the assortment of goods to be sold. The right mix and choice of merchandise along with the right pricing would play an important role in the selection of a particular store by the customer, and it is a key differentiating factor. It is a dynamic activity that has to be in tune with customer needs, and it also has implications for the topline and bottom-line of a retail store. If the planned stocks sell within one week, with the same money the store owner can buy stocks for the next week and so on, and he can rotate or turn the stocks four times in a month. If he sells the same stock in 15 days, then the stock turn achieved will only be twice a month. While with four times stock turn, the store may get an 'x' amount of profit, with the lower stock turn of two times, the profit goes down by a half.

Buying for a retail store is a critical function of merchandise management. The process of buying begins with the formation of an idea of what to stock up the store with, in what quantities, in what price and when. The planning of buying starts with budgeting exercise of how much to invest in what categories of products. The next step is to identify the vendor for each product, negotiate prices and buying terms and then finally buy the products. Retailing often involves a number of products and SKUs, which make this task difficult. Purchasing function has to work in co-ordination with sales for doing the timely replenishment of sold items. Above all, the purchasing function needs to take care of the needs and wants of customers who should be able to access products when they would want to without facing a no-stock situation in the store. An excess stock situation is more dangerous because any inventory pile up would lead to a cash-strapped scenario where the storeowner may be left with no money to buy more products. That may lead to a vicious impact of less business in the store resulting in the presence of obsolete products in the store for which customers may not find any need any longer. The buyer can clear such held up stocks by marking them down and selling at lesser prices so that cash is released to buy more products to satisfy customers.

Need for Multitasking People in Retailing

People in retailing, especially those with small- and medium-sized stores, ought to learn to do multitasking. They must be good salespeople who can double-up as merchandising and buying resource. They have to also know how to take care of cash and accounting in the store. Marketing the store is yet another key function, which is usually carried out by salespeople as part of their multitasking role in small retail stores. The storeowner may disseminate information about the products and offers to the catchment by means of brochures printed in the vernacular language and distribute them through paper and milk run vendors to households. Salespeople can put up daily offers and best prices through shelf-talkers pasted on the shelves in the right places where discounted merchandise may be kept. The store promotion may also be done by the store sales team in local events and large gatherings of customers in the town. It may be expensive for start-up and small retail stores to have a dedicated person for every function.

Manpower Planning Processes

Since manpower costs form a major part of costs for the retailer, the decision on how many people it should have is critical. The manpower plan has a bearing on the standards of performance, productivity and profitability. Most importantly, it may affect the kind of service that a retailer may like to offer. Very often, retailers are so busy managing operations that the key issue of manpower planning is ignored. They often fail to understand that a proper plan can improve while saving costs. The following factors have to be considered while planning manpower for a small store organization: (a) The number of customers to be attended needs to be taken into consideration in a high footfall retail store. In a busy store, more than one person may be needed to serve customers on time, (b) The nature of roles, tasks and timing like shifts need to be considered for determining how many people to be employed in the retail store and (c) Above all, the ratio of manpower cost to turnover which is the most significant criterion needs to be considered while deciding the number of employees for a small- and medium-sized retail store organization.

Family Roles in Small- and Medium-sized Retailing in India

The retail landscape in the area of small- and medium-sized retailing in India is large, and a majority of these retail stores are managed by family. Family members would be involved in performing all the functions of retailing in the small retail stores. If each member in such stores performs certain functions and roles, performance accountability could be ensured and results could be better. In the case of just two members of the family, perhaps a husband and wife or a father and son run the business, both of them need to be adept in all the functions they perform, with a conscious decision to gain competencies in the demanding functions of retailing such as efficient selling, dedicated customer service, prudent buying and planned pricing. While employing people in the phase of expansion, small retailers ought to take necessary care to become a mentor and train such people to work with commitment like an entrepreneur himself. The employee needs to be trained to 'own' all that he does so that there is greater accountability in what he/she is expected to deliver for the growth of the organization.

Choosing the Right People and Practices: Shri Kannan Departmental Store, Coimbatore

Reminiscing about the days when Thanushgaran 'Annachi' (as he is popularly known _ meaning elder brother in Tamil) began his first small grocery retail store in 1976 in Erode, Tamil Nadu, he says,

> It was a time when I wanted to start the retail store with an extreme desire to win in life. Energetic as I was, I wanted to do the business of running a grocery retail store, and the grocery retailing business I found in my blood itself.

He also goes on to say,

> It was not an easy business. I had to go to the market getting up as early as 4 a.m. every day for purchasing goods for the store. I had to

fix the prices for every item in such a way that mine could emerge as a loving store to the neighbourhood consumer. Then later, I had to get ready to work in the store till late at night and on many days beyond midnight.

Soon his grocery store became popular in the Erode town itself, leave alone the neighbourhood.

Thanushgaran Annachi had just dropped out of college post his pre-university education, before he could graduate. He travelled from his native village near Tiruchendur in the then Tirunelveli district of Tamil Nadu, and as a young man went by himself to Erode in Periyar district, a distance of around 400 km seeking to do some worthwhile business to grow. He says, 'Winning in the retail business was my only goal then and I would work tirelessly as I do now too, to see for myself that every item was purchased at the proper price and sold to customers rightly'. He had a penchant to know most of his customers. He says that he would personally know them and their families by grabbing every opportunity to speak with them. He says, 'My relationship with the customers was so good that my customers trusted my store completely and I was very careful to always give my customers the highest quality of products at the best prices'.

The retail business in his first store called 'Somanur *Maligai Kadai*' grew by leaps and bounds. Thanushgaran Annachi attributes the success of Somanur *Maligai Kadai* to careful planning of gross margins by efficient pricing and clever procurement. He says that he paid personal attention to buying goods for the store. He would not only go to the market himself as mentioned earlier, but he would look for competitive distributors, vendors and wholesalers who would offer the best price. He would also look for opportunities to do speculative buying of staples knowing when prices would go up and make his plan to buy when prices were low. At the same time, he would see that inventories were controlled and the store was not overstocked, maintaining short buying cycles. He says that in the earlier stages of growth, he was purely dependent on internal accruals of profits. He admits that the store's growth began to happen the moment he started maintaining books of accounts, which eventually helped him raise bank funds. Banks would only see the books of accounts to understand sales and profits so that overdrafts could be approved. He obtained term loans too to use the funds for expanding categories in the store.

When Somanur *Maligai Kadai* was established, initially, it was less than 1,000 square feet in size and, later, expanded to almost about 8,000 square feet, which also included a wholesale business. The wholesale business catered to many small retail stores in and around Erode. In 1985, he says he opened a fancy and gifts store in 600 square feet. This new format of business also performed well and the store could quickly win many loyal customers. Annachi says, 'My efforts to give genuine products identifying customer needs and their timeliness paid off well and that fuelled the growth of my store'. The store was known as 'Sangeetha Shopping Centre', named after his daughter. As divine influence would have it, when he returned from a pilgrimage trip from Tirupathi, he says, he rechristened his shop, having integrated both the *Maligai Kadai* and the Fancy Store into one entity called 'Shri Kannan Departmental Store'. The store became a large one with a wholesale 'business-to-business' (B2B) division to cater to smaller stores in the vicinity and to institutions such as schools, colleges and hospitals in Erode. Identifying potential for establishing a Shri Kannan Departmental Store in Coimbatore, Mr Thanushgaran opened a shop there in a large format in Trichy Road. He believes in the customer-centric philosophy of providing the maximum number of categories any middle class customers and families would need so that they do not have to go anywhere else to shop. In Coimbatore, he expanded the product categories to include fresh vegetables, groceries, sweets and snacks, convenience goods, gifts, stationery, dairy products, cosmetics, electronics, furniture and furnishings, clothing, travel accessories and medicines in a one-stop-shop format. The growth of Shri Kannan Departmental Stores was so phenomenal that he expanded the store-spread in Coimbatore to Ramnagar, Mettupalayam Road, Ganapathy, Kuniamuthur, Singanallur, Saibaba Colony, etc. From the little acorns grow mighty oaks and, thus, the seed of the retail business sown in Somanur, Erode, in a small *maligai* store has now grown to a big chain of retail stores in Tamil Nadu. The organization has now expanded, in addition to Coimbatore and Erode, to the towns of Salem, Gobichettipalayam, Dindigul, Karur, Komarapalayam, Madurai, Pollachi, Tirupur, etc. A 2,500-people-strong organization, the company is marching towards achieving a turnover of ₹500 crore per year soon.

Mr Thanushgaran chooses young people and trains them to carry out various functions, mainly merchandising, store operations and accounting. The store managers and department managers are internally groomed and nurtured and people in senior positions have more than 10 years' experience in the company. Annachi personally trains people in the store on displays and sales. Whenever he visits each store, he spends time speaking to his people to motivate them towards being close to the business with passion.

Here's a clear insight into the best practices of merchandising in Shri Kannan Departmental Stores: The company during its growth phase started integrating backwards into manufacturing and preparation of whatever items were possible in the merchandise mix. Shri Kannan Department Store in Coimbatore has a back-end food and snack manufacturing facility on the outskirts of the city, where items from packed 'chappatis' to 'murukku' and 'chakli' are made. The facility has an in-house bakery with facilities to make bread, biscuits, cookies, pastries, etc., a kitchen for various packaged snacks, a repacking unit for grocery and a supply chain hub for all its private label products such as masalas, oils, ayurvedic products and Indian medicine products. In addition to this facility, they operate on a merchandising concept called 'the house-supported brands'. House-supported brands are those that give good margins. The store does not only analyse the top-selling items but also the top-yielding items in every category. The top-yielding national brands are given preference for displaying the products at eye-level in the planogram to promote sales. Others are pushed down or higher for customers to pick and choose products if they still want them. In every category, such analyses are made and such yielding brands are taken in with confidence to co-promote and cocreate growth opportunities. As the organization operates stores in locations in Tamil Nadu, this manufacturing hub takes into account the localized requirements of all the operating catchments around the towns and takes up the responsibility of supplying to the stores on time using the company's own logistics facility. The organization focuses on a cash and carry format also. Such learning may be useful for every retailer to create a clear winning localized merchandising strategy. Customers would always want to remain in their 'roots' as far as their food habits are concerned, though they may often try out many other varieties of foods.

Passion is a key aspect with which Mr Thanushgaran works. He always keeps himself close to the business and makes visits to all the stores whenever possible. He looks at every category of products manufactured by the company or sourced from other manufacturers or bought from vendors and distributors. He meets his key people to know and follow up with gross margins and operating expenses of every store periodically. His leadership and attention to detail on merchandising, margins and store operations stand Annachi in good stead and enable him to take the company to the next level of growth into various other key towns of Tamil Nadu. Thanushgaran Annachi has two daughters, and after completing her studies his first daughter, Sangeetha, shadows him now in the business, getting inducted to co-manage the company along with him.

Key Takeaways from Kannan Departmental Store

- Develop customer intimacy_that's the key attribute for the success of any retail business.
- Maintain proper books of accounts to obtain bank funding to grow and expand business.
- Integrate backwards to make/prepare easy-to-make snack food items.
- Repack grocery in own name.
- Create back-end manufacturing facility to prepare possible SKUs.
- Join together in fruitful alliances with other manufacturers, vendors and distributors and buy products at lesser prices.
- Create a distinctly attractive local merchandise mix.
- Keep expenses (especially rental expense) low.

Bibliography

Baisya, Rajat K. 2013. *Branding in a Competitive Marketplace*. New Delhi: SAGE Publications.

Bisen, Ankur, Pragya Singh, and Ashima Anand. 2013. *E-tailing in India: Unlocking the Potential*. Technopak Report. New Delhi: Technopak Advisors.

Biyani, Kishore, and Dipayan Baishya. 2007. *It Happened in India*. New Delhi: Rupa & Co.

Bright, Bill. 1997. 'Committed to Marriage'. In *A Life of Integrity*, edited by Howard Hendricks. Sisters, Oregon: Multnomah Publishers.

Green, Karen. 2017. *Recipe for Success: The Ingredients of a Profitable Food Business*. Leicester, UK: Troubador Publishing.

Mukherjee, Arpita. 2005. *FDI in Retail Sector in India: A Report by ICRIER and Ministry of Consumer Affairs, Government of India*. New Delhi.

Muherjee, Arpita, Parthapratim Pal, Saubhik Deb, Subhobrota Ray, and Tanu M. Goyal. 2016. *Special Economic Zones in India: Status, Issues and Potential*. New Delhi: Springer.

Nath, Rachna, Akash Gupt, et al. 2012. *The Indian Kaleidoscope: Emerging Trends in Retail*. A FICCI–PWC Report. New Delhi.

Nayak, Amar K. J. R. 2011. *Indian Multinationals: The Dynamics of Explosive Growth in a Developing Country Context*. Hampshire, UK: Palgrave Macmillan.

Sabnavis, Madan, and Darshini Kansara. 2017. *Indian Retail Industry—Structure & Prospects*. CARE Research Report. Mumbai: CARE Ratings.

Schroeder, Carol L. 2002. *Specialty Shop Retailing: How to Run Your Own Store*. New Jersey: John Wiley & Sons.

Singhal, Arvind. 2016. *Nine Key Trends Impacting India in Next Nine Years*. Technopak Report. New Delhi: Technopak Advisors.

Spector, Robert. 2005. *Category Killers: The Retail Revolution and Its Impact on Consumer Culture*. Massachusetts: Harvard Business School Press.

Underhill, Paco. 2008. *Why We Buy: The Science of Shopping*. Barcelona, Spain: Orion Mass Market.

Vedamani, Gibson. 2017. *Retail Management: Functional Principles and Practices*. Pearson Education. Chennai.

Walmart. 2015. *Q&A with Doug McMillion*. Excerpts from Walmart's Annual Report. Walmart Blog, Arkansas, USA.

Web Portals

https://blog.walmart.com/business/20150422/q-a-with-doug-mcmillon-seeing-the-future-through-customers-eyes, accessed on 3 October 2017.

http://www.business-standard.com/article/companies/future-group-s-kishore-biyani-expects-33-growth-in-retail-business-in-fy19-118012400936_1.html, accessed on 28 January 2018.

https://www.businesstoday.in/current/economy-politics/baba-ramdev-balkrishna-and-patanjali-success-reasons/story/237282.html, accessed on 8 November 2017.

http://www.chitalebandhu.in/t/About%20Us, accessed on 18 November 2017.

https://corporate.shoppersstop.com/corporate/history-new.aspx, accessed on 12 March 2017.

http://dipp.nic.in/sites/default/files/pn5_2016.pdf, accessed on 4 August 2016.

http://dipp.nic.in/sites/default/files/CFPC_2017_FINAL_RELEASED_28.8.17_1.pdf, accessed on 2 September 2017.

http://differenttruths.com/business/they-sat-smiling-a-journey-from-under-the-neem-tree-to-supermarket/, accessed on 2 June 2017.

https://economictimes.indiatimes.com/industry/services/retail/hm-clocks-in-rs-700-crore-sales-in-nine-months/articleshow/60870770.cms, accessed on 3 October 2017.

https://www.flipkart.com/about-us?otracker=undefined_footer_navlinks, accessed on 28 January 2018.

https://www.franchiseindiaweb.in/patanjali-franchise-products-dealership/, accessed on 4 February 2018.

http://www.futuregroup.in/about-us/about-group.html, accessed on 28 October 2017.

www.gibsonvedamani.blogspot.in, accessed on 24 August 2017.

https://www.ibef.org/industry/retail-india.aspx, accessed on 15 May 2017.

https://www.idfreshfood.com/our-food/vada-batter/, accessed on 22 January 2018.

https://www.indiainfoline.com/article/capital-market-ipo-centre-new-issue-monitor/khadim-india-117103000267_1.html, accessed on 17 December 2017.

http://www.indiaretailing.com/2016/04/12/fashion/westside-fashion-comes-alive, accessed on 11 September 2017.

http://www.jashn.in/aboutus, accessed on 12 November 2017.

https://www.khadims.com/about/, accessed on 18 December 2017.

http://www.livemint.com/Companies/Ei0DISs04h3aN02eLA1vTN/Sri-Sri-Ravishankars-Sriveda-Sattva-eyes-franchisee-route-t.html, accessed on 20 January 2018.

http://www.msmeonline.tn.gov.in/definition.pdf, accessed on 4 June 2016.

http://www.mywestside.com/WebPages/InnerPages/aboutus.aspx accessed on 30 January 2018.

http://www.referenceforbusiness.com/history2/52/Safeway-PLC.html, accessed on 10 May 2016.

https://www.retaildive.com/news/walmart-to-sell-modcloth-bonobos-only-on-jet/449660/, accessed on 2 September 2017.

http://www.shrikannan.com/aboutus.php, accessed on 11 September 2017.

http://www.srisritattva.com/en/about-us/, accessed on 2 January 2018.

http://www.starbucks.in/media/Starbucks%20Brings%20Mobile%20Payment%20to%20India%20with%20its%20Mobile%20App%2014%2002%2017_tcm87-27902.pdf, accessed on 4 April 2018.

https://successstory.com/companies/flipkart, accessed on 28 January 2018.

http://www.thehindubusinessline.com/companies/Hatti-Kaapi-cheering-cuppa/article20736275.ece, accessed on 16 June 2016.

http://www.thephoenixmills.com/company-history.asp, accessed on 12 February 2015.

http://www.theweekendleader.com/Success/2583/success-with-coffee.html, accessed on 2 February 2017.

http://www.theweekendleader.com/Success/2365/ma-baker.html, accessed on 18 November 2017.

http://www.viveks.com/AboutUs.aspx & http://www.viveks.com/ArticlesDesc.aspx, accessed on 6 October 2015.

https://www.youtube.com/watch?v=czLhQDV-Fx4, Speech by Mr T. Thanushgaran, Chairman and MD, Shri Kannan Departmental Store on YouTube, accessed on 15 November 2016.

https://www.youtube.com/watch?v=h2TImf-x-aU, accessed on 22 January 2018.

About the Author

Gibson G. Vedamani holds a PhD in retail management (from Symbiosis International University, Pune). He is Founder and Partner, Retail Solutions and Learning Technologies LLP, Mumbai. He is the former founding CEO of Retailers' Association of India (RAI). He has played a key role in establishing RAI in India as the country's recognized professional retail body. He has shared the 'Great Indian Retailing Story' in many conferences and forums including the ones hosted by National Retail Federation, USA, and Columbia Chamber of Commerce, South America.

Dr Vedamani currently serves as a Director on the Board of Gem and Jewellery Skill Council of India as an NSDC nominee. He also sits on the boards of a few companies as Non-executive/Independent Director besides being a Trustee/Advisory Board Member of a few educational and higher educational institutions. Before his tenure as CEO of RAI, he served in leadership positions in Reliance Webstore, Piramyd Retail, Bhojsons (Nigeria), Shoppers Stop, Bata India, Aurofood and Godrej Consumer Products.

An author and writer on topical retailing, Dr Vedamani has also published two more books on retailing and many articles in reputed newspapers, journals and magazines. He is passionate about teaching retail management, and he is a guest faculty at the Jamnalal Bajaj Institute of Management Studies, Mumbai, Prin. L. N. Welingkar Institute of Management Development and Research, Mumbai, GRD Institute of Management, Coimbatore, and Christ Institute of Management, Pune. He is the recipient of the Dewang Mehta Award for the best teacher in retail management, FICCI's Retailers' Retailer Award and IBS Award for the best contribution to the retail sector in India.

'This book is a must-read for organizations that are looking to positively engage with the millennial generation. It boldly attempts to define the rules of engagement for a generation that will reshape our future.'

Kiran Mazumdar-Shaw
Chairperson and Managing Director, Biocon

A Fascinating Eye-Opener into the Life of Y!

For special offers on this and other books from SAGE, write to marketing@sagepub.in

Explore our range at
www.sagepub.in

₹495

The Life of Y: Engaging Millennials as Employees and Consumers
Debashish Sengupta

Paperback
978-93-866-0274-9

Prices subject to change

"Analysts, benefit from Ramesh and Kuldeep's research and help your organization further its goals."

Jeremy Shapiro
Executive Director, HR, Morgan Stanley

Transforming Organizations Using HR Analytics

For special offers on this and other books from SAGE, write to marketing@sagepub.in

Explore our range at
www.sagepub.in

₹395

Prices subject to change

Paperback
978-93-860-4241-5